BICYCLE METALLURGY
FOR THE CYCLIST

by

DOUGLAS HAYDUK

Front cover: This 100% sterling silver bicycle, 3" long, is handmade in Italy. A limited quantity of these bicycles are available by special order from the author. Photography by Michael Lichter.

Copyright © 1987 by Douglas Hayduk

First Printing, July 1987

For additional copies, contact:
  Douglas Hayduk
  604 Marine St.
  Boulder, Colorado 80302

All rights reserved. This book, or parts thereof, may not be reproduced in any form without permission in writing from Douglas Hayduk, 604 Marine St., Boulder, Colorado.

Printed in the United States of America
by Johnson Publishing Co., Boulder, Colorado.

ISBN 0-9618977-0-8
Library of Congress Catalog Number: 87-081490

"At last, there is a book that tells the story of metallurgy of the bicycle as it is, without all the advertising gimmicks and hypes. For all of those involved in the cycling industry, this book is a must!"

--- Julian Edwins, Edwins Cycle Corporation
Owen Sound, Ontario, Canada

Camera ready copy for this book was prepared by **Debra Bruck Document Publishing,** 2305 Glenwood Drive, Boulder, Colorado, (303) 442-6871. Original copy was printed entirely at 300 dots per inch (DPI) on a Cordata LP300X laser printer. Artwork was scanned at 300 DPI on a Datacopy 730 scanner, and then enhanced using ZSOFT's PC Paintbrush and Media Cybernetics' Dr. HALO D.P.E. software. The final copy was prepared using the Xerox Desktop Publishing Series: Ventura Publisher Edition software.

ACKNOWLEDGEMENTS

The author would like to express his gratitude to the many, both companies and individuals, who provided input and assistance for this undertaking. My most sincere thanks and appreciation goes to my parents, Alfred G. and Vivian S. Hayduk. Special thanks also goes out to the following:

Julian Edwins, Edwins Cycle Corp., Owen Sound, Ontario, Canada

Department of Metallurgy, Colorado School of Mines, Golden, Colorado

Martin Chenoweth, Martin Custom Cycles, Grand Junction, Colorado

Eugene A. Sloane, Bicycle Industry Consultant, Vancouver, Washington

Richard Gängl, Gängl Custom Bicycles, Golden, Colorado

TABLE OF CONTENTS

PREFACE viii

INTRODUCTION x

CHAPTER I: METALLURGY AND MATERIALS SCIENCE ... 1

    METALS 2

        Steel 12

        Nonferrous Metals 16

            Aluminum 16

            Titanium 19

            Magnesium 20

    COMPOSITES 21

    FAILURE OF METALS
            (FRACTURE AND FATIGUE) 28

CHAPTER II: FRAMESET MATERIALS 37

    STEEL FRAMESETS 41

    NONFERROUS FRAME MATERIALS 53

        Aluminum Frames 53

        Magnesium Frames 55

        Titanium Frames 57

- COMPOSITE FRAMESETS 59
- COMBINATIONS OF MATERIALS 64
- FRAME GEOMETRY 66

CHAPTER III: BICYCLE FRAME CONSTRUCTION 70
- LUGS, BRAZING, AND WELDING 70
  - ADHESIVE BONDING and MECHANICAL JOINING 76
  - PLATING and ANODIZING 77

CHAPTER IV: BICYCLE COMPONENTS 81
- RIMS and SPOKES 82
- HANDLEBARS, FREEWHEELS, CHAINS, ETC. 86

CHAPTER V: FUTURE DIRECTIONS 89

GLOSSARY: TERMS AND DEFINITIONS 95

REFERENCES AND ADDITIONAL READING 110

PERIODIC CHART OF THE ELEMENTS 111

Preface

BICYCLE: A vehicle consisting of a metal frame mounted upon two wire-spoked wheels with rubber tires, a seat, handlebars for steering, and two pedals by which it is driven.

METALLURGY: The science and technology of creating useful objects from metal.

CYCLIST: One who rides a bicycle.

This book presents a brief overview of metallurgy and its involvement in the bicycle industry. The book's objective is to give cyclists an unbiased presentation of the structural materials encountered in the world of bicycles. This book is not intended to be an introductory course in metallurgy or materials science. A thorough explanation of the fundamentals of metallurgical engineering would necessarily get quite complicated and involved. Therefore, the complicating details of this science are intentionally left out in order to keep the text brief and understandable. A more indepth presentation would only serve to confuse of bore most readers. A more comprehensive look at metallurgy and bicycles can be obtained from one of the references listed at the end of the book.

It is not the intent of this book to recommend one material over another; say, for example, aluminum frames over steel frames. It is left to the reader to decide which material is best suited for his or her needs. This book is written as an unbiased report of the subject matter, leaving out hunches and opinions so that the text will not unjustifiably influence the reader.

In order to achieve the simplicity and brevity of this book, it was necessary to make occasional generalizations and simplifications about particular topics. However, all attempts were made to maintain a high degree of accuracy.

Some of the metallurgically-related details which primarily concern framebuilders are not discussed in this book. These include: specific braze alloys and properties of each alloy, fluxes, chemical stripping and cleaning of metals, etc. These details are thoroughly addressed in the several good framebuilding books out in print.

INTRODUCTION

Fact or Fiction? Science or Mythology?

Consider the following statements:

"The front fork loses its elasticity when chromed."

"Those rims are dark gray, and therefore, heat treated."

"The frame failed because the metal crystallized and became brittle from overheating during brazing."

"My frame has become soft and mushy after a whole season of racing it."

"Chrome plating of a bicycle frame is bad."

These are some of the more common beliefs held by cyclists and others involved in the bicycle industry. Are these statements all true? Only some of them true? Only some of them partially true?

It will take the bicycle enthusiast only an afternoon of running around to several bike shops to see that there are a variety of stories and rumors told about the pros and cons of frames, rims, and other bicycle components. Very technical terminology is used, often erroneously, and this only seems to confuse even the technical-minded cyclist.

TECHNICAL TERMS

cold-forged components
heat treatable alloys
chrome-moly steel
TIG-welded
hard anodized finish

Today's bicycle industry is full of technical jargon that is not common to the average consumer's vocabulary. Most of the time these terms have very descriptive scientific meanings. Sometimes though, these seemingly high-powered words are fabrications of manufacturers meant to impress the consumer and set their products apart from those of competitors. The salesperson in a bike shop will then try to favorably impress the customer with those "high-tech" terms that are passed on to him or her. They themselves may have little or no understanding of these buzzwords describing that new light weight bicycle. The consumer is, more often than not, baffled by it all. At the end of this book is a very helpful section, **Terms and Definitions**, which briefly defines most of the terms used in this book and in the cycling community.

Be warned that you cannot believe everything heard or seen in print. There is a great deal of literature out there that is in error or is misleading and is largely corrected in this book. The author could spend the next ten or so pages illustrating this point by recounting examples of erroneous statements and explanations of bicycle metallurgy. The following, a direct quote from an expensive book on high-tech bicycles, will serve to demonstrate the last point:

"The more heat used in brazing, the greater the strength loss in the steel and the greater likelihood of the formation of crystalline structures in the grain of the metal."

Though this explanation may sound somewhat reasonable, it is in fact very incorrect and misleading. It is the sincere hope of the author that this book will serve to clear up these type of misunderstandings.

History and Background of Bicycle Metallurgy

Everyone has certainly heard of the Stone Age, the Iron Age, and the Bronze Age. These are periods of world history that were greatly shaped and influenced by the science of materials, especially metallurgy. In an analogous way, the history of bicycle development has been largely dependent upon discoveries and developments in the field of metallurgy.

The early development of bicycles took place in the forty years between 1860 and 1900. These bicycles were made largely of wood and iron. Modern materials like steel and aluminum alloys had not yet been invented. Wood proved to lack the strength needed for high performance and man had no ingenious ways to restructure and treat wood to make it better. Therefore, these early bicycles were made almost completely of iron.

As manufacturing progressed, new ways of making iron stronger by the addition of carbon and other elements were being discovered. As steelmaking technology was developed, steel soon displaced iron as the primary material for bicycles. T. I. Reynolds Ltd., the famous English bicycle tube producer, best known for

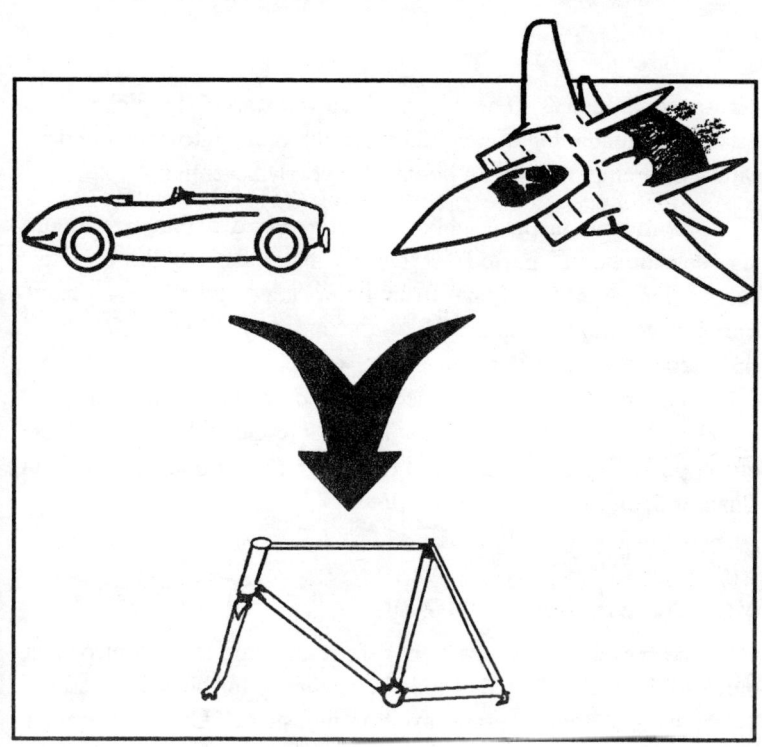

their "Reynolds 531" tubing, started manufacturing light weight bicycle tubes from steel in the 1890s. The tube butting process was patented by Alfred M. Reynolds exactly 100 years ago, back in 1887.

From the late Twenties up until the Sixties, there was only limited effort spent on furthering materials technology for bicycles. The world was more concerned with automobiles, airplanes, and wars. Then, as greater technology in the aluminum industry was developed, and as bicycle designers recognized the importance of weight savings, aluminum alloys began to replace steel. Titanium metallurgy was developed in the Fifties and Sixties, and this new wonder metal showed great promise for the bicycle industry. Graphite fiber composites were invented in the Sixties and an ever-increasing use of these fantastic materials had begun in the aerospace industry. The bicycle industry started to pick up on these new technologies and incorporate them into their designs with the coming of the bike boom in the early Seventies.

Presently, we in the Eighties are in a very dynamic, revolutionary, developmental period for bicycle materials. In the past few years, aluminum has gone from being considered as an exotic frame material to a standard of the industry. Composites have risen from their status as an exotic, mysterious, and very unaffordable material to a reasonable choice of materials for high-end bicycles. What is the future holding for bicycle technology? Some of the possibilities are discussed throughout this book, especially in Chapter 5, entitled **Future Directions**.

Borrowed Technology

Since bicycles were invented before automobiles and airplanes, much of the technology developed specifically for bicycles was used by the early automobile and aviation industries. Credit for much of the initial development in these two industries belongs to the bicycle. It is a well-known fact that the Wright Brothers operated a bicycle shop from which their legendary aircraft emerged to take to the skies at Kitty Hawk, North Carolina, making world history.

Unlike with aerospace firms, bicycle manufacturers and designers must operate from profits on their sales. They don't get awarded multi-million dollar government contracts for research and development. It is interesting to realize that today the automotive and aerospace industries are repaying their debt to the bicycle industry. Much of what is new or "high-tech" to the bicycle was originally developed for a specific aerospace application, often after years of extensive research. The most notable examples are the uses of titanium, composites, and adhesive bonding techniques.

Organization Of This Book

Chapter I is an introduction to metallurgy and materials science. After a presentation of some basic fundamentals of metallurgy, this chapter is organized according to individual alloy systems: steel, aluminum, titanium, and magnesium. A section on composites is also included in Chapter I. Little mention is made of specific bicycle applications in this chapter. With the foundation and perspective offered in Chapter I, the specific applications of metallurgy to bicycles, Chapters II through V, are more easily comprehended. The glossary, **Terms And Definitions**, located at the back of this book, is alphabetized for quick reference.

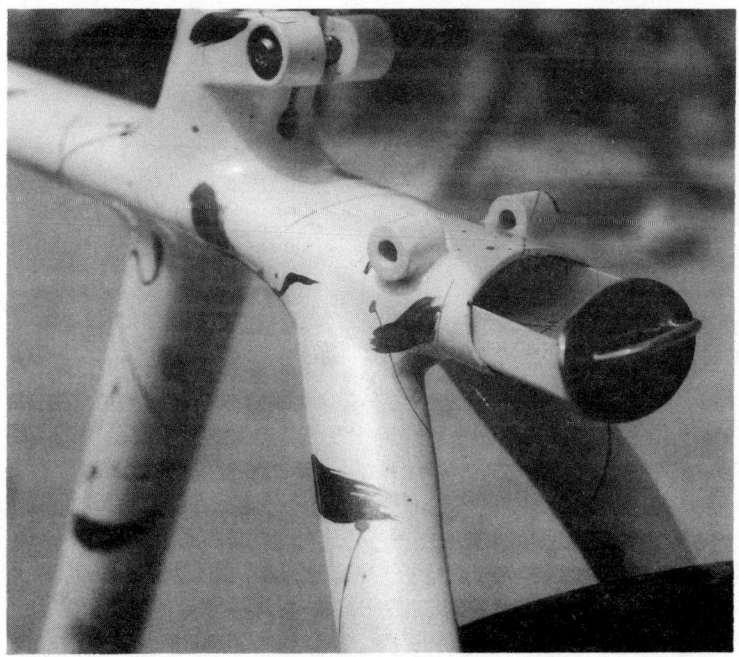

Accessory drawer on the Moots tandem. Courtesy of Kent Ericksen and Moots Cyclery, Steamboat Springs, Colorado.

CHAPTER I

METALLURGY AND MATERIALS SCIENCE

While it may be obvious to everyone that most bike frames are made of some kind of metal, it's not so clear just what is meant when a particular material is classified as a metal. When referring to bike frames and components, the terms *aluminum alloy*, *titanium alloy*, or just plain *alloy*, will certainly be mentioned. This section is devoted to giving the cyclist a very basic understanding of metals and their alloys. Additionally, some fundamentals of composites are also presented in this chapter.

Materials Science

Materials science and engineering is a very broad field. There is a whole set of encyclopedias written specifically on this subject. The engineered materials can be classified in various ways. If we survey the entire field of engineering materials, we find that there are three principal groups:

- Metals: steel, copper, cast iron, etc.
- Ceramics: glass, brick, cement, etc
- Plastics and other high polymers: polyethylene, rubber, etc.

What about composites? Where do they fit in this system? Well, composite materials consist of various combinations of metals, ceramics, and polymers.

Without a doubt, the metals are the primary materials used in the bicycle industry. Why? Simply because metals offer the engineering properties necessary for bicycle design at a reasonable price.

METALS

Ti   **Mg**   **Fe**   **Al**

What is a Metal, and *What is Metallurgy?*

Metals are elements in the Periodic Table of the Elements. Every material thing in the universe is made from the elements of the Periodic Table (or Periodic Chart), shown on Page 110. The periodic table is an organization of the basic building blocks, called elements, that are found on this earth which combine with each other to create plants, food, water bottle cages, rear derailleurs, and our own bodies. Each element can be referred to by its abbreviated chemical symbol, consisting of one or two letters (hence, Cr-Mo steel is chrome-molybdenum steel).

These 104 elements, some of which are very familiar to us, and some which are rarely heard of, can be divided into metals and nonmetals. Metals all have particular common characteristics that are very different from the nonmetals. There are some elements, called metalloids, that have characteristics of both metals and nonmetals. Approximately three-fourths of these hundred-plus elemental atoms are classified as metals. However, in the world of cars and bicycles, coins and steak knives, only a dozen or so of these metals are much used.

The nature of metals. Some of the characteristic properties common to most metals are:
- They are strong, yet tough and ductile.
- They are opaque and lustrous.
- They are good conductors of electricity.
- They conduct heat effectively.
- They are chemically active and combine readily with both metallic and nonmetallic elements.
- They have crystalline microstructures.

Note: Words like microstructure, toughness, and ductility are defined in the section **Terms and Definitions**.

Metallurgy is the science and technology of metals. As a branch of engineering, metallurgy is concerned with the production of metals and alloys, their adaptation to use, and their performance in service. A metallurgist is one who performs this work. Metallurgy has played an important role in the history of civilization. Metals were first produced by man more than 6000 years ago and ever since that time, new discoveries of metals and their use has dramatically changed the way in which people exist on this planet. Look at the effect that the two metals, gold and silver, have had on human civilization. And where would the transportation and construction industries be without steel and aluminum alloys?

Metal versus Alloy

What is an alloy? An alloy is defined as a substance having metallic properties and being composed of two or more chemical elements of which at least one is a metal. Not everything made of metal is an alloy. For example, sodium chloride (NaCl), or common table salt, is composed of a metal (sodium) and a nonmetal (chlorine). However, salt doesn't have metallic properties and consequently, is not an alloy. Pure metals are not alloys because they consist of a single metal element. Very few of the metals are used in their pure form because pure metals usually don't have the necessary properties for engineering uses.

Technically, the word *metal* refers to a single metallic element and *alloy* refers to a combination of metals. However, these words are frequently used interchangeably. Within this book, one will be chosen over the other when it is important to distinguish one from the other. When *aluminum* or *titanium* is mentioned, this usually refers to *aluminum alloys* and *titanium alloys*. In the cycling world, the term *alloy* is commonly used to refer to any of the aluminum alloys.

Impurities in Alloys

All metals and alloys will contain small amounts of other metals or nonmetals (sulfur, phosphorus, silicon, etc.). These are impurities that come from the metal production. Sometimes the presence of impurities is of no consequence. But often, these impurities can strongly affect the metal's properties, usually in a negative way. Corrosion resistance and weldability are highly dependent upon impurity levels for many alloys. Because of these considerations, metal producers will often make special grade alloys that have very low impurity levels. They cost more, but they may make a significantly better end product. Cleanliness (lack of impurities) is a quality of alloys that may differ between alloys from different producers. Some examples: 304L stainless steel (the "L" is for a low carbon version of 304 stainless steel); AZ91D magnesium alloy (the "D" indicates a high purity grade of AZ91).

All Metals are Crystalline and Consist of Microscopic Grains

The most distinguishing characteristic of metals is the way that the atoms are arranged in definite geometric patterns when they solidify from the molten (liquid) state. There are fourteen dif-

5 BICYCLE METALLURGY FOR THE CYCLIST

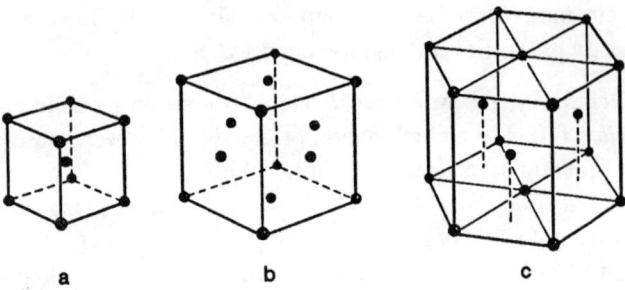

The three most common crystal lattices: (a) Body-centered cubic; (b) Face-centered cubic; and, (c) Hexagonal close-packed.

ferent crystal structures possible and each metal can form in one or more of these crystal arrangements. The particular crystal structure of a metal has a lot to do with its mechanical properties.

The crystalline structure of a metal is sometimes evident to the naked eye, as in the case of an piece of iron pyrite (*fools gold*). Most often, however, the crystalline structure is not obvious to the naked eye. That's because the crystals are in the form of microscopic grains (not unlike grains of salt). A round glob of solidified braze metal sure doesn't look like it has any sort of crystalline pattern to it. But if polished and put under a microscope, the small crystal grains of metal could be seen.

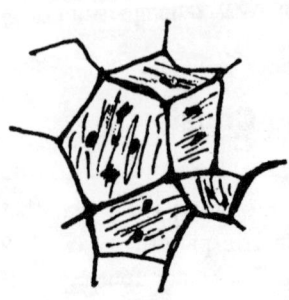

The grain size is a very important characteristic of a metal, and partially determines its mechanical properties. A metallurgist can treat metals in various ways that change the size and shape of these grains in order to produce different mechanical properties. Generally, for good mechanical properties, fine grains are better than large grains.

Metals Are Characterized By Physical and Mechanical Properties

Physical Properties

Physical properties of a metal are those that are relatively insensitive to the structure of the metal. In other words, physical properties aren't changed by heat treating, working into tubing, sheet, or other physical forms. For bicycle design, the most important physical properties are density and modulus of elasticity. These two properties remain relatively constant for each particular alloy system. For example, all aluminum alloys have approximately the same modulus of elasticity and density, as do all steel and titanium alloys.

Density

Density is defined as the weight of a material for a given unit volume, usually reported in pounds per cubic inch or grams per cubic centimeter. Densities are used to compare the weight of different materials. Density of a metal is constant, no matter what is done to the metal. One might think that by hammering, rolling, or forging a metal, the density would increase. However, this just doesn't happen. In order of lighter to heavier, densities of the metals used for bicycles are:

    magnesium alloys -- .065 pounds per cubic inch
    aluminum alloys -- .100 lb./in.^{3}
    titanium alloys -- .165 lb./in.^{3}
    steel alloys   -- .285 lb./in.^{3}

7 BICYCLE METALLURGY FOR THE CYCLIST

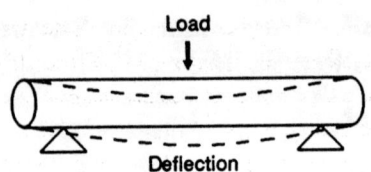

Modulus of Elasticity

Design engineers are vitally interested in the stiffness of the materials they work with. They must know how much deflection (strain) can be expected from bicycle frame tubes in actual service. Modulus of elasticity, also known as Young's Modulus, or "E", describes how stiff a material will be. In other words, stiffness of a material is best described by its modulus of elasticity.

Modulus of elasticity is essentially the same for all alloys within a particular alloy system. By this logic, a bicycle frame made of plain carbon steel would be equally as stiff as the same frame made of Reynolds 753 with an equivalent tube wall thickness and diameter. While this may be so, there are other important characteristics, like strength, that would not be the same.

Note: While *rigidity* and *modulus of elasticity* are often used interchangeably, the rigidity of a metal structure also takes into account the geometric configuration of the metal. Hence, a stiff material will be rigid only if it is properly designed for rigidity.

The different metals used for bicycles have the following elastic moduli:

magnesium alloys -- 6.5 million pounds per square inch

aluminum alloys -- 10.5 million psi

titanium alloys -- 17 million psi

steel alloys -- 30 million psi

This tells us that for tubes with the same wall thickness and diameter, steel tubes will be roughly three times as rigid as aluminum tubes. Therefore, steel is much more stiff than aluminum. However, aluminum, titanium, and magnesium can all be used to make more rigid tubes by simply increasing wall thickness, tube diameter, or both. This of course means more weight. That explains why the weight of all high quality, light weight metal frames, whether steel, aluminum, or titanium, weigh within a pound of each other.

Note: The properties of composites are highly dependent upon their method of construction, orientation of fibers, and direction of testing. More is said about this in the **Composites** section of this book.

Mechanical Properties

Mechanical properties are the specific characteristics describing a material's behavior when a force is applied to the material. This is exactly what we want to know when considering whether or not a material would be good to make a bicycle frame or component out of. Mechanical properties can be measured for different materials and used to compare the suitability of these materials for a particular use. Some common mechanical properties are:

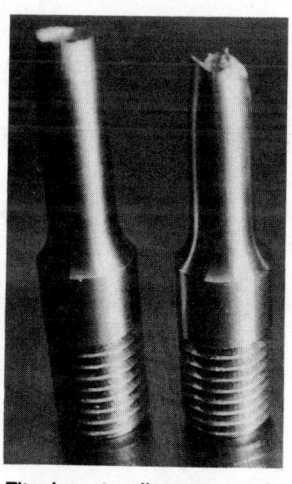
Titanium tensile test specimen pulled to fracture.

yield strength	**ultimate tensile strength**	**hardness**
fracture toughness	**fatigue strength**	**ductility**

9 BICYCLE METALLURGY FOR THE CYCLIST

These and other related terms are all defined in the section **Terms and Definitions**, found at the end of this book.

Unlike physical properties, mechanical properties of a material are very dependent upon the condition of material. For instance, the same steel tube can have one strength when carefully heat treated and then later have a much lower strength if heated differently (annealed). Forging, rolling, extruding, or stamping processes can all change the strength of a metal.

The mechanical properties of an alloy can be altered in one of two ways: 1) heat treatment, and 2) mechanical working. Together, the two combined factors are referred to as thermomechanical processing.

Heat Treatment

When a metal is alloyed with other elements, these elements can combine in different ways, depending upon how they are heated and cooled from room temperature up to the melting point. Metallurgists have very exact sequences of heating and cooling operations that will give an alloy a desired set of mechanical properties. While not all metals can be heat treated, some metals can be heat treated in several very different ways. Heat treating is different for steel alloys and aluminum alloys. Where putting a piece of aluminum alloy in a home cooking oven may strengthen the aluminum, this relatively low temperature would do absolutely nothing to steel.

Since many alloys can be heat treated to higher strength levels, the mechanical properties of a particular alloy can have more than a single value. There will be a reported value for each condition of heat treatment. For these alloys, the heat treated condition must also be mentioned. As an example, for the common aluminum alloy 6061, the heat treated condition must also be mentioned in order to know its mechanical properties. Therefore, this alloy will be reported as 6061-O, 6061-T4, 6061-T6, etc. The letter and numbers following the alloy name will stand for a specific heat treatment. Some alloys, particularly the steels, will have the heat treatment written out following the alloy number designation. For example: 4130 steel-annealed, 4130 steel-quenched and tempered.

Mechanical Working

In order for a metal to become a bicycle rim or a brake lever, the metal must be put into the desired shape by some means. Unless the part is cast into a mold having the desired final shape, the metal will be mechanically worked into its final form. Rolling, forging, extruding, stamping, are all different mechanical working processes used to fabricate various components of a bicycle. If this working process is done at low temperatures (less than 1/2 of the metal's melting temperature), the metal will usually harden and gain strength. This phenomenon is called *work hardening*, *strain hardening*, or *cold working*. For many alloys, including steels and aluminum alloys, cold working is a very important means of strengthening the metal.

Processing Methods: Cast or Wrought

How does an alloy go from being molten metal to a shiny new bicycle component or a frame tube? This is known as process metallurgy, the science and art of the processes for making things out of metal. There are two basic ways to make a metal product; either as a casting or as a wrought product.

Casting is fairly straightforward process. The molten metal alloy is poured into a mold that is the shape of the final part and allowed to solidify. This casting may be heat treated and/or machined to achieve the final shape, but it is nearly a finished part once it is cast. There are many different casting techniques; sand casting, die casting, permanent mold casting, and investment casting are the most common. Some of the high quality bicycle frame lugs are cast products, usually fabricated by precision investment casting.

11 BICYCLE METALLURGY FOR THE CYCLIST

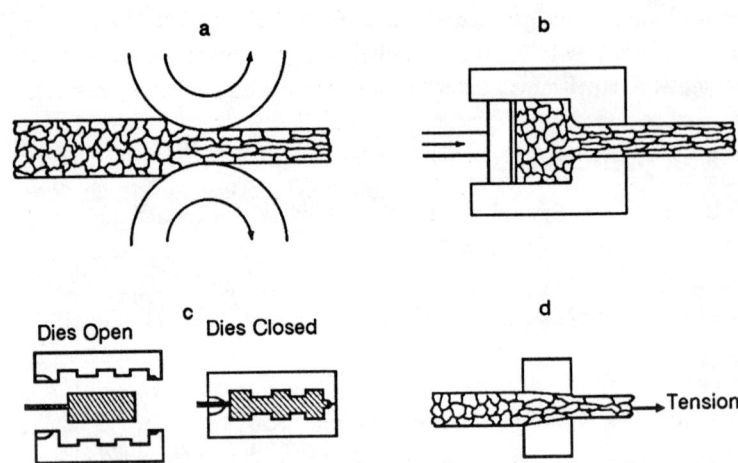

Methods for work hardening during processing: (a) Cold rolling bar or sheet; (b) Cold extrusion; (c) Cold forming, stamping, forging; and, (d) Cold drawing.

Wrought products are those that are first cast into a big block of metal (called an *ingot*) and then worked in one of many ways to achieve a final shape. Most bicycle components are wrought products, including the frame tubing. The term wrought is not often heard because it's not very descriptive. The final processing is how the part is usually described. For example, stamped, rolled, rolled and welded, machined, forged, forged and machined, extruded, and drawn, are all possible wrought processes.

For each of the steel, aluminum, titanium, and magnesium alloy systems, there are alloys developed specifically for either wrought applications or for castings. Some alloys can be used for either castings or wrought products.

Which Metal Processing Method Produces The Best Product?

There is no single and absolute answer to this question. Each of the processes mentioned in the previous paragraph, including casting, have their pros and cons. There are several factors for determining how a metal part will be produced: cost, desired mechanical properties, surface finish, the particular alloy used, etc. Some processes are very cheap and lend themselves to mass production, while other processes, like investment casting, must be performed on an individual basis, making them quite expensive to produce.

Naming Systems for the Different Alloys

4130

Ergal

Chrome-Moly

6061-T6

Each of the different alloy systems; steel, titanium, aluminum, magnesium, etc.; have their own naming system. Numbers or numbers and letters are usually used to designate a specific alloy. Unfortunately, there is no universal system used by all countries. European and Japanese alloy designations may sometimes be different. What makes things more confusing is that the metal manufacturers often have their own tradename for a particular alloy. Some examples of this are: Dural, Avional, Ergal, Zicral. These are all manufacturers names for different aluminum alloys. Similarly, Reynolds 531, Tange Mangaloy, and True Temper T1, are all tradenames that come from steel bike tube producers.

Steel

Steels constitute over 90% of the metallic materials used for structural purposes, whether for bike frames or for skyscrapers. There are literally thousands of different compositions of steel that have been made and used for a particular purpose. Despite this complexity, there are only a handful of steels used for bicycles.

What Is Steel?

Steel is a combination of iron and carbon, primarily iron, with percentages of other elements unavoidably present or intentionally added to achieve a specific quality or characteristic.

All steels are based on the element iron (chemical symbol Fe). Iron is by far the least expensive of all of the metals and, next to aluminum, the most plentiful. Pure iron itself is used only for relatively few special applications. Most iron is used in the form of plain carbon steels. Carbon is the most important addition that gives steel its high strength. For the low strength steels, less than 0.2% carbon is added. However, for high strength steels, up to 2% carbon can be added. This may not seem like very much carbon but this carbon makes a world of difference in the resulting mechanical properties of steel. Additionally, carbon content in steel is measured by weight, not volume, and since iron atoms weigh four times as much as carbon atoms, there is actually more carbon atoms in the steel than the percentage would suggest.

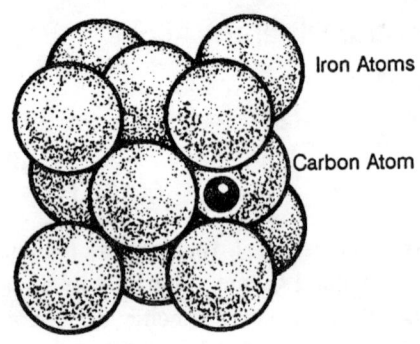

The following are some common metals that may be added to steel to give it particular properties: manganese, chromium, vanadium, nickel, molybdenum. Classification of steel is based on chemical composition. The most widely used system is the SAE-AISI system (Society of Automotive Engineers - American Iron and Steel Institute). A four number designation is given to a particular steel. Some common examples are: 1020, 4130, 4340. Stainless steels are an exception, using only three numbers.

Steels can be grouped into the following general categories:

plain carbon steels   **alloy steels**   **stainless steels**
tool steels   **cast irons**

However, only the plain carbon steels, low alloy steels, and stainless steels are much used in the bicycle industry.

Plain Carbon Steel

Also known as carbon steel, this is the most inexpensive and widely used steel for all industries and uses. Carbon steels can be further divided into three groups, which are:

Low carbon steel -- 0.10% to 0.25% carbon. Also called "mild steel". Because of its low cost, ease of fabrication, adequate strength, excellent finishing characteristics, and its compatibility with other materials and coating processes, low carbon steel has very widespread use in most all industries, and for most consumer goods. Tensile strength (UTS) of low carbon steels is less than 80,000 psi. 1020 steel, containing 0.2% carbon, is the most common low carbon steel.

Medium carbon steel -- has a carbon range of about 0.3% to 0.6% and less than 1% manganese. These steels have more strength than low carbon steel. They can be heat treated to strengths as high as 150,000 psi UTS.

High carbon steel -- greater than 0.6% carbon and up to 1% carbon. Steels in this group are more costly to make, have poor formability, and poor weldability.

Although plain carbon steels can be produced in a great range of strengths at relatively low cost, their properties are not always adequate for all engineering applications. They generally cannot be strengthened to greater than 100,000 psi. They have poor corrosion resistance for many applications and they can't be fully hardened. For these and other reasons, alloy steels have been developed.

Microalloyed steels: In recent years, the microalloying of plain carbon steels with small amounts (rarely exceeding 0.1%) of elements such as niobium, titanium, and vanadium (Nb, Ti, and V) has achieved a great improvement in their mechanical properties. The addition of these elements also improves the properties of the steel after brazing or welding.

Low Alloy Steel

Like the carbon steels, these steels contain carbon, manganese, and usually silicon. However, low alloy steels also contain from 1% to 5% of one or more of the following alloying elements: nickel, chromium, molybdenum, and vanadium. These steels are heat treatable to very high hardness and strength in excess of 200,000 psi UTS. Sometimes these steels are referred to simply as *alloy steels*.

4130 steel, a chromium-molybdenum low alloy steel, is the most widely used steel for high quality bicycle frame tubing. This steel contains 1% chromium, 0.2% molybdenum, and 0.30% carbon, (as well as small amounts of silicon, manganese, and phosphorus). So, as you can see, while this is a "chrome-moly" steel, it is still about 95% iron. Depending upon how this steel is heat treated, the tensile strength of 4130 can range from 100,000 psi to 200,000 psi.

High Alloy Steels (Stainless Steels)

All of the previously mentioned steels have relatively small amounts of alloying additions to the iron base. The high alloy steels have well over 5% total alloying elements added for special purposes. The most common of the high alloy steels is the family of stainless steels. Stainless steels contain at least 10% chromium and as much as 10% nickel. The most distinguishing feature of stainless steels is the very high corrosion resistance achieved without painting, plating, or otherwise coating. That's why stainless steels are widely used for the medical, food service, and chemical industries. Nuts, bolts, axle skewers, bearings, and other small bicycle components may be fabricated from stainless steel.

A three number designation is used for the stainless steels. *SS* or *stainless* following the numbers indicates a type of stainless steel. Common types of stainless steel used for bicycle components are 301 SS, 302 SS, 304 SS, 410 SS, and 440 SS. The general term *18-8 Stainless* is often used and refers to one of the 300-series stainless steels which contain 18% chromium and 8% nickel.

Nonferrous Metals

Nonferrous literally means "without iron", or in other words, "not made of steel". Aluminum alloys, titanium alloys, and magnesium alloys are the nonferrous candidates for bicycles. Their biggest attraction is that they are lighter weight (have lower densities) than steel alloys. This is the big reason that these alloy systems are very important in the aerospace industry.

Aluminum

Aluminum ranks second only to steel in the metals market. Aluminum is light in weight, yet some of its alloys have greater strength than structural steel. Aluminum is alloyed to achieve different properties. Pure aluminum lacks the strength needed for bicycle frames and components. There are many different alloys of aluminum out on the market, each produced for a different end use. Like the steel alloys, aluminum alloys are classified by the major alloying elements added. All wrought aluminum alloys are given a four-letter designation from the following code developed to make it easy to recognize the type of alloy:

BICYCLE METALLURGY FOR THE CYCLIST

Code	Major Alloying Element(s)	Heat Treatable?	Example
1XXX	Essentially pure Al	No	1060 (99.6% Al)
2XXX	Copper	Yes	2014 (4.5% Cu)
3XXX	Manganese	No	3003 (1.3% Mn)
4XXX	Silicon	No	4032 (12.5% Si)
5XXX	Magnesium	No	5052 (2.5% Mg)
6XXX	Magnesium & Silicon	Yes	6061 (1% Mg, 0.6% Si)
7XXX	Zinc	Yes	7075 (5.6% Zn)

Note: This code system is for the wrought aluminum alloys. A different three-digit code system is used for the cast aluminum alloys.

The **XXX** or **000** following the first number indicates a series of common alloys. Within each series, there is an exact number for each specific alloy. The alloy 6061 is pronounced "sixty-sixty-one". Other alloys are pronounced in a similar manner. While there are many different alloys within each series, only one or two alloys in each series are widely used in the bicycle industry.

The 2XXX, 6XXX, and 7XXX series aluminum alloys can be heat treated to achieve higher strength, while the others must rely on cold working to attain higher strength. Heat treatment allows aluminum alloys to achieve their highest possible strength. Since the mechanical properties of the heat treatable alloys are so dependent upon the heat treated condition, an additional prefix called the *temper designation* or *temper condition* should always be attached to the alloy code. The most common temper designations, listed in order of increasing strength, are:

- O   annealed
- T4   solution heat treated and aged at room temperature
- T6   solution heat treated and aged at elevated temperature

Note: Other temper designations are frequently seen and are defined in any textbook on engineering materials or aluminum alloys.

The highest strength temper is the -T6 condition. The 7XXX series are the highest strength aluminum alloys. The most common 7XXX alloy, 7075, in the -T6 temper, has a yield strength of 73,000 psi and an 83,000 psi ultimate tensile strength. The alloy 7178, used for True Temper's T2 bicycle tubing, has a maximum yield strength of 78,000 psi and a maximum ultimate tensile strength of 88,000 psi. This is very high strength for the aluminum alloys, but is only half the strength achieved by high strength steel bicycle tubing.

For all aluminum alloys, including the heat treatable alloys, cold working is a very effective means of strengthening the metal. There is a prefix attached to the non-heat treatable aluminum alloys that have been cold worked. This designation is a capital "H" followed by a number, indicating the degree of cold work. Examples are: 5052 H3, 3004 H18.

Welding Aluminum

A common fabrication method is to start with annealed (-O temper) aluminum and cold work and/or heat treat to achieve the desired mechanical properties. High temperature processes like welding will remove the strengthening effect of prior heat treatment. So, if aluminum in the -T6 temper condition is welded, the metal in the welded zone will be left in the range of the annealed condition to the -T4 temper condition. In order to return the entire part to its strongest condition, a controlled re-heat treatment process is necessary.

Aside from the heat effects on temper condition, aluminum is generally not difficult to weld by the TIG process. The non-heat treatable alloys are easily welded. However, of the heat treatable alloys, only the 6XXX series alloys have excellent weldability. Some of the lower strength 2XXX and 7XXX series alloys can also be welded. The alloys 7005 and 7039 (or alloys very similar in composition to these two aluminum-zinc alloys) are new discoveries to welded aluminum bicycle builders. Frames welded from 7005 or 7039 are used in the as-welded condition. Those alloys that do not have good weldablility, like 7075 or 7178, are usually joined by riveting or adhesive bonding. Brazing is not generally performed on any of the aluminum alloys.

Aluminum Heat Treatment

Heat treatment of aluminum is a two-part process. The first is solution heat treatment, achieved by holding the entire part up near its melting temperature followed by immediate immersion in a coolant (this is called *quenching*). The second part is artificial aging, accomplished by heating to approx. 300-400° F for a specific time. Natural aging refers to aging that occurs at room temperature, bringing the aluminum to the -T4 temper condition. The alloy 7005 in the as-welded condition will naturally age to the -T4 condition, bringing back 90-95% of the original strength. Those frames made of 6061-T6 must be re-heat treated after welding because the alloy 6061 does not naturally age as well as 7005 does.

Titanium

Titanium alloys have been developed only recently, since just after World War II. Titanium's low density, high strength, and excellent corrosion resistance make it attractive for use as a structural material. The chemical symbol for titanium is Ti.

Titanium's density is approximately midway between that of steel and of aluminum. Additionally, its modulus of elasticity is approximately halfway between steel's and aluminum's. This gives titanium a stiffness-to-weight ratio very close to both steel and aluminum. Titanium alloys can be heat treated to strengths almost as high as the high-strength steels.

Like aluminum and steel, titanium is alloyed with other metals for higher strength. Chromium, iron, tin, aluminum, vanadium, zirconium, and molybdenum, are all common alloy additions to titanium. There are many different titanium alloys available for different applications, especially for aerospace use. However, since only two or three alloys are used in the bicycle industry, the different titanium alloy groups will not be presented here. By far, the most commonly used titanium alloy is Ti-6Al-4V, called "six-four titanium". This means that it is 90% titanium with 6% aluminum and 4% vanadium. Other commonly used titanium alloys are Ti-5Al-2.5Sn and Ti-3Al-2.5V.

Titanium alloys can be heat treated in ways similar to steel. There are no code designations for heat treatments like those used for aluminum alloys. Welding does not severely degrade the mechanical properties of the titanium alloys used in the bicycle industry. Therefore, the titanium structures fabricated by welding can be used in the as-welded condition with little or no loss in mechanical properties (no re-heat treatment is necessary). Titanium, most commonly welded by the TIG process, must be done in an atmosphere free from air. This means either flooding the hot or molten titanium with a non-reactive gas like argon, or doing the welding in a closed chamber filled with argon gas. Any oxygen or nitrogen that gets absorbed by the molten weld metal causes severe embrittlement of the titanium.

Titanium alloys are indeed more expensive than steel and aluminum alloys, but not prohibitively so. For top-of-the-line bicycle components, the weight savings is often considered to be worth the added cost.

Magnesium

Magnesium (chemical symbol Mg) is a metallic element much like aluminum but has only 2/3 the density of aluminum, and 1/4 the density of steel! Magnesium has the honor of being the world's lightest structural metal.* The cost to produce magnesium alloys is on the same order as both steel and aluminum. Consequently, the alloys of magnesium are competitive with those of aluminum. Magnesium alloys can't achieve the high strength that aluminum and steel alloys do, but due to its low density, the specific strength (strength-to-weight ratio) is comparable to steel's or aluminum's. Magnesium finds its widest application in the aircraft industry, where its excellent strength-to-weight ratio can be used to full advantage.

Like aluminum, the magnesium used for structural purposes is not pure magnesium metal, but is alloyed with other metals, usually aluminum and zinc. The most commonly used magnesium alloy, AZ31, contains 3% aluminum and 1% zinc. For castings, the two common alloys used are AZ63 and AZ91, containing 6% aluminum, 3% zinc, and 9% aluminum, 1% zinc, respectively.

* Beryllium (chemical symbol Be) is a lighter metal than magnesium with very limited structural use in critical aerospace applications. Its high cost and fabrication difficulties keep beryllium from becoming a pratical material for bicycle applications.

COMPOSITES

In the aerospace world, composites have been used successfully for over 25 years. Composites are presently the fastest growing of the advanced structural materials for the aerospace industry. In the cycling world, composites are very new. Only a few different carbon fiber/epoxy resin framesets were available in the 1970s. Technology developed by the aerospace industry has provided a tremendous baseline and spin-off to non-aerospace applications, including the bicycle industry.

Large-scale composite use in the bicycle industry is just beginning. *What makes these materials so desirable? Are they practical for use in the bicycle industry? And just what is a composite, anyway?*

"IT'S A GOOD IDEA FOR THE WHEEL, BUT I'D PREFER A CARBON FIBER FRAME."

What are Composites?

The whole subject of composites is quite complex. The term "composite" can refer to anything from steel-reinforced concrete to carbon fiber reinforced aluminum alloys (metal-matrix composites). The list of candidate materials for use in composites is almost limitless. However, for the bicycle industry, the term *composite material* refers to a combination of many high-strength reinforcement fibers surrounded by and held together by a matrix of epoxy or other polymer resin.

We are all familiar with fiberglass and its thoroughly developed use as a structural material (fishing poles, tennis rackets, Corvette auto bodies, etc.). Well, fiberglass is a composite material consisting of glass fibers in an epoxy resin matrix. However, fiberglass structures are just too heavy and not strong and rigid enough for bicycle frames. By substituting carbon fibers in place of glass fibers, both stronger and lighter weight structures are produced.

Composite Fibers

For bicycles, the fibers used are either entirely carbon or carbon fibers blended with other very high strength fibers like Kevlar. The term *graphite* is often used instead of *carbon*. Graphite and carbon are one and the same. Graphite simply denotes the specific form of carbon used for composites. Diamonds are another form of carbon very popular with female cyclists. Kevlar is a DuPont tradename for their very high strength aramid (inorganic polymer) fibers. There are two different types of Kevlar: Kevlar 29 and Kevlar 49. The difference between the two is that the latter has a modulus of elasticity twice that of the other. Even so, these Kevlar fibers don't have as high a stiffness as the carbon fibers. The addition of Kevlar to the composite structure give better compressive strength and increased damage tolerance. This means that the Kevlar will help hold the composite together during heavy impact loading that would otherwise cause catastrophic fracture of the structure. Carbon and Kevlar fibers start out life as a long filament wound around a spool, not unlike fishing line.

The Composite Matrix

The matrix is responsible for the integrity of the composite. It binds the reinforcement fibers together to allow effective distribution of loads, as well as to protect the flaw- or notch- sensitive fibers from self-abrasion and externally induced scratches. The matrix also protects the fibers from moisture and corrosion. The most widely used matrix for carbon fiber composites is the family of epoxy resins. These epoxy resins start out in liquid form and are hardened, or *cured*, usually by heating in an oven after the composite is put together.

Carbon fiber composite material is often used in the form of *prepregs*. This term refers to carbon fiber cloth or fabric that is pre-impregnated with resin before assembling into structure. Prepregs are used for the hand layup method of composite fabrication.

Composite Tubing and Molded Composites

There are two fundamentally different methods for making composite bicycle frames. The most common and familiar method is by joining composite tubing into a traditional diamond-shaped frame by using lugs. The other method, molded composite construction is very new to the cycling world.

Tube Fabrication

Tube fabrication and assembly is, by far, the cheaper and more common method of composite frame building. Frames constructed by this method look very similar to traditional steel frames. The diameter and thickness of tubing, and method of joining are the significant differences in composite tubing frames from steel frames.

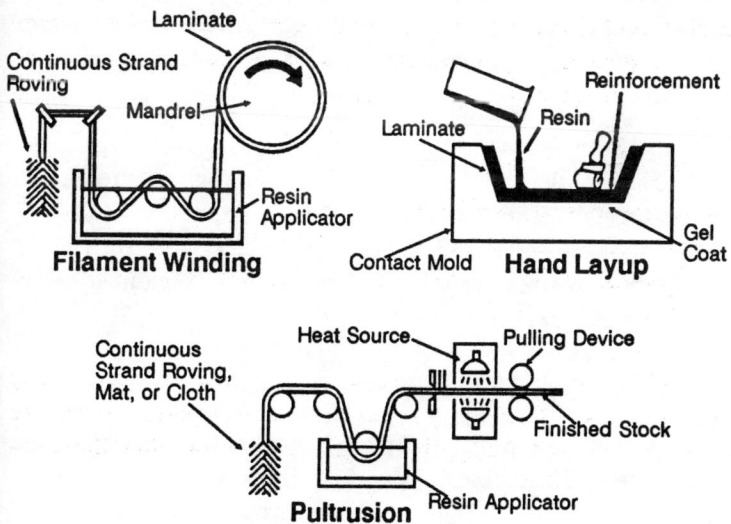

Hand Layup, Filament Winding, and Pultrusion

Fabrication of bicycle tubes can be accomplished by different methods. Hand layup, filament winding, and pultrusion are the common ways of making bicycle tubing.

Hand layup involves manual placement of fiber-reinforced mats, fabric, or pre-impregnated tape, over a tubular-shaped mandrel. This mandrel may be removed after the composite cures, or alternatively, the mandrel may be designed to be left intact as a part of the tube structure. Although very labor intensive, hand layup offers the maximum in design flexibility and the minimum investment in fabricating equipment. Hand layup tubing can also be fabricated by a molding process which utilizes an outer die to compress the uncured fiber/resin layups around the inner mandrel.

Filament winding is accomplished by weaving the strands or filaments of fibers (carbon, Kevlar, etc.) into a woven fabric around a removable cylindrical mandrel. The resin matrix is applied to the fibers either before winding, after winding, or both. The tube is then placed in an oven for curing. Curing is the process that hardens the resin matrix. The weaving pattern can be varied to give different properties at any point along the tube. This ability to "taylor-make" a tube is an important advantage for filament winding.

Pultrusion involves pulling the fiber cloth or strands through a resin bath, then drawing the impregnated material through a die which gives it the tubular shape and controls the reinforcement/resin ratio. The die is usually heated to initiate the curing process. Final curing is done by pulling the tube stock through an oven. Very high strengths are possible due to the high fiber orientation and concentration.

Molded Composites

The molded composite technique, also known as matched-die molding, uses the simplest composite fabrication method, hand layup. As previously mentioned, hand layup involves the manual placement of fiber reinforcement mats or strips of fabric or tape into an open mold the shape of a bicycle frame. The mold, usually made of plaster, has two identical halves. Several layers of fabric (either carbon fiber, Kevlar fiber, or both) are built up in each mold half, with extra thickness and specific fiber orientation in areas of greater stress. One big-name composite framebuilder, Brent Trimble, uses approximately 25% carbon fiber fabric and 75% Kevlar fabric in his design. Epoxy resin matrix is either applied to the fabric during this process or the resin may be already present in the fibers (prepregs). Metal inserts are placed where needed (bottom bracket, seatpost, heatset, etc.), and the two halves are removed from the mold, pressed together, and bonded. The big advantage of composite molding over tubular construction is that the structure is continuous. There are no joints or lugs that make the structure's properties discontinuous. Additionally, you can "taylor design" the frame to get the necessary strength and stiffness where most needed.

Mechanical Properties of Composites

As mentioned earlier in the section on physical and mechanical properties of metals, composite properties are very dependent upon the fabrication method. They are highly directional (dependent upon the direction tested) and commonly will not be constant within a structure. A single tube can have different properties at different points along its length.

The mechanical properties of composites can not be directly compared with those of metals. Composites don't have yield strengths, constant densities, or constant moduli of elasticity. Each fabricated structure is different. This is why a table of mechanical properties, like the one included in this book for the different alloys, isn't included here.

Choosing a high performance matrix and fiber is important to composite properties, but perhaps even more important is the way in which these components are arranged. Each composite manufacturer can put the fibers and matrix together in different proportions and different geometric patterns. Fiber composite tubes with all fibers oriented longitudinally have very high longitudinal tensile strength but suffer in other loading situations (twisting, or torsional loading, for example). This is why for bicycle tubing, different layers of fibers must be oriented at varying orientations with respect to the longitudinal axis.

Joining of Composites

Unlike the metals, composites can not be welded or brazed. The resin matrix just will not stand up to very high temperatures. Presently, the only way for composites to be joined is either mechanically or by adhesive bonding.

Damage of Composites

Fatigue and fracture characteristics are very much different for composites than for metals. In the next section it will be seen that fatigue of metals depends upon alternating stress cycles that will initiate a tiny crack, which will then slowly propagate through the metal until failure. This explanation does not hold for composites. In general, composites are highly resistant to fatigue problems.

When composite structures are subject to impact, they can internally split and delaminate. This means that damage to a composite structure can go undetected by visual examination of the surface. This may have serious implications for a bicycle frame that has been crashed hard.

Corrosion Resistance

Generally, properly coated carbon-fiber/epoxy-resin composites are highly resistant to corrosion. Uncoated composites can be subject to long-term deterioration due to weathering, but the composite tubes used for bicycles are coated, usually with polyurethane. There has been concern with the effects of ultraviolet radiation upon composites. However, this deterioration occurs over many years and isn't something to be terribly worried about for bicycle frames. As a sure measure of UV damage prevention, the polyurethane enamel that is commonly used to coat composite framesets acts as a barrier to ultraviolet radiation.

Additionally, there is a potential for serious corrosion problems when a composite is joined directly to metals, as in the case of carbon fiber tubing to aluminum lugs or sleeves. This is known as galvanic coupling and galvanic corrosion. The seriousness of galvanic coupling in bicycle frames is not exactly known. Some feel that the problem is very minor while other frame designers account for any potential problem in their joint design. Insulating the interface between the carbon and the metal is the only sure way to eliminate the possibility of galvanic deterioration. The adhesives used to bond the frame tubes together act as a barrier to electrical contact between the carbon and the metal. The effectiveness of the insulating adhesive depends largely upon the joint construction. Advanced Composite Technology Co., of Golden, Colorado, has had their frameset joints tested according to aerospace specifications for galvanic coupling. The results showed a zero potential for any detrimental galvanic action.

FAILURE OF METALS (FRACTURE AND FATIGUE)

A metal part or assembly is considered to have failed under one of three conditions:

a) When it becomes completely inoperable.

b) When it is still operable but is no longer able to perform its intended function satisfactorily.

c) When serious deterioration has made it unreliable or unsafe for continued use.

So, as you can see, failure doesn't always imply "a broken part". For the cyclist, failure may occur in the form of a worn-out bearing race, or as a catastrophic failure of a handlebar. It is the catastrophic failures, however, that often carry serious consequences. Fortunately, most cyclists don't often have to deal with this type of failure on their bicycle.

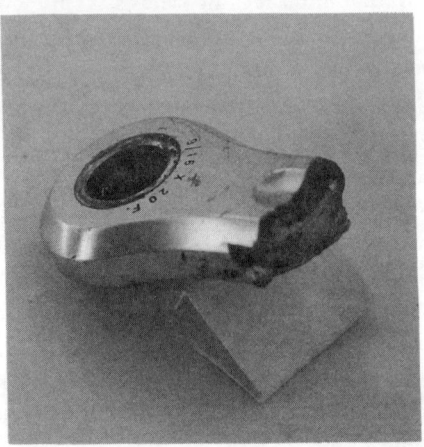

Crankarm failed by fatigue. Dark, flat fatigue region and light, rough overload region are evident.

Failure Analysis

Occasionally, one hears about the catastrophic failure of someone's bike frame. When this happens, analysis should be conducted by an expert to prevent future failures. Additionally, the manufacturer or framebuilder should most certainly be notified. Bicycle frames should not fail under normal circumstances. One that does, needs corrective action taken for subsequent framesets. The exact cause of failure can most always be determined with proper failure analysis. Failure analysis is a very well developed branch of metallurgy used to determine what failed, how the failure occurred, why it occurred, and how corrective action can be taken.

A metallurgist can usually tell, just by looking at a metal fracture surface, how the metal failed; whether by fatigue, overload, hydrogen embrittlement, or one of the other mechanisms of metal failure. The accompanying photograph shows a typical fracture surface for a steel part failing by fatigue. This photo shows that the crack was initiated at the point of highest stress (a stress raiser), indicated by point A, slowly grew through region B, and then suddenly, fractured (broke apart). The rough appearance of region C is what will lead an uninformed person to incorrectly believe that "the metal started to crystallize, became brittle, and caused the failure". We know that this explanation is erroneous. Metals are crystalline in the first place. The rough part of the fracture surface is caused by fast, unstable cracking of the metal after the fatigue crack slowly grew to a critical size. Discoloration from corrosion can often be seen on region B as a result of long term exposure to the atmosphere.

Fracture surface of stainless steel threaded connector. Failure occurred due to fatigue.

As mentioned above, failures can be classified by the way in which the metal failed, called the failure mechanism. Some of the different failure mechanisms are: fatigue, overload, corrosion, stress-corrosion cracking, hydrogen embrittlement.

Aluminum fracture toughness test specimen.

Fatigue

Fatigue is perhaps the most common failure mechanism for broken bicycle components. Fatigue failure is the failure of a material due to cyclic (repeated) tensile stresses. The size of the stress that will cause failure of a metal after a specified number of cycles is known as the fatigue strength. Steels will have a stress level, known as the endurance limit, below which there will never be any problem with fatigue. In other words, if the stress is kept below the fatigue endurance limit, a part will be able to endure an infinite number of stress cycles (i.e., have an infinite life).

The cyclist skeptical of aluminum as a frame material will state that aluminum does not have a fatigue endurance limit and is subject to early fatigue failure. It is indeed correct that aluminum does not have an endurance limit. As the number of loading cycles increases, the critical fatigue strength decreases. Therefore, an aluminum part will be designed for fatigue by specifying a very conservative number of cycles, often 500 million.

In terms of miles ridden or years used, how long is a fatigue life of 500 million cycles? Well, for a frameset, let's assume that the bike is ridden for 2 hours per day, seven days a week, every week of the year. If it is assumed that the rider pedals at 90 rpm, never coasts, and is always pedalling hard, then the following calculations can be made:

$$\frac{1 \text{ stress cycle}}{\text{revolution}} \times \frac{90 \text{ rev.}}{\text{minute}} \times \frac{60 \text{ minutes}}{\text{hour}} \times \frac{2 \text{ hours}}{\text{day}} \times \frac{365 \text{ days}}{\text{year}} =$$

3.9 million cycles of loading per year

And then, assuming that the rider pedals in an average gear of 42x15, the total distance ridden per year is:

$$\frac{3.9 \text{ million cycles}}{\text{year}} \times \frac{1 \text{ revolution}}{\text{cycle}} \times \frac{42}{15} \times 3.14 \times 27" \text{ wheel}$$

$$\times \frac{\text{ft.}}{12 \text{ inches}} \times \frac{\text{mile}}{5280 \text{ ft.}} = 14,600 \text{ miles per year}$$

The assumptions for riding conditions made here are extremely conservative. Actual cycles and mileage would be considerably less than these figures. This example shows that for a frame properly designed for 500 million cycles, the fatigue life is nearly "infinite". However, fatigue life prediction is not really as simple as the last example. Estimating the cyclic stresses of a bicycle's fork is not as straightforward as the last example. There are many uncertainties inherent in analytical predictions of fatigue life. Thus, a large safety factor should be incorporated into any bicycle design.

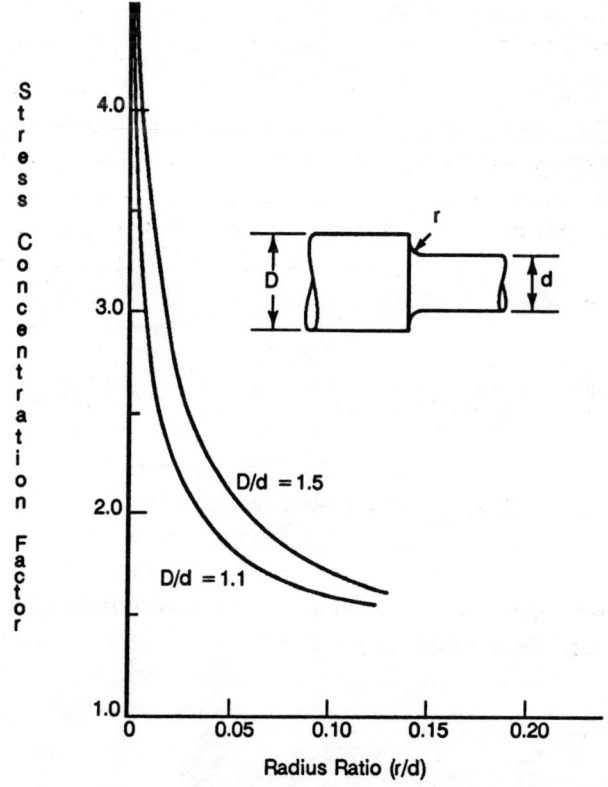

Stress Raisers

A stress raiser is a change in the surface coutour of a part that causes a localized increase in stress. This is best illustrated by these sketches of the stress distributions in a loaded spindle or axle. When a part is loaded, the material carries that constant load throughout the material. However, stress is concentrated wherever there is a section change, or geometric discontinuity, in the part. This location of highest stress is where fatigue failures will occur. Typical stress raisers are threads, grooves, notches, and holes.

Pedal Spindles Under Bending Load

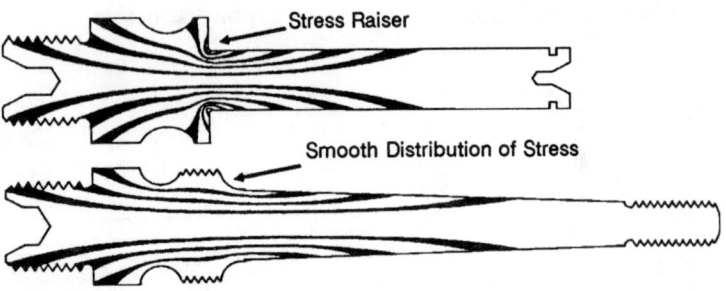

Many stress raisers are found in bicycles. Pedal spindles, hub axles, bottom bracket spindles, frame lugs, and crankarms are all parts that have stress raisers in their design. All of these parts have been known to fail by fatigue in a catastrophic manner, resulting in injury to the rider. Frame lugs and holes drilled into the tubing for water bottle cages or cables also act as stress raisers. If a component or frameset is properly designed around its stress raisers, there is usually no problem with fatigue failure. Still there are quite a few bicycle components that fail due to the careless introduction of stress raisers into the design of a frame or component. Often, these stress raisers are unnecessary and can be easily remedied. The most simple way to lessen the severity of a stress raiser is to design smooth transitions into the material. This may be as easy as careful machining of a part or filing of a lug.

Bicycle Failures

Unfortunately, there has been very little documented work done in bicycle failure analysis. Some general causes of failures that occur in the bicycle industry are: design inadequacies, manufacturing processes not conforming to the design, materials selection problems, operating problems, maintenance problems, unanticipated loading. The incidence of failure by one of the above-mentioned mechanisms is not well known. This is because unless serious injury is involved, the cyclist will usually repair or replace the failed part, climb back on the bike, and resume riding. Manufacturers aren't always notified about failures of their framesets or components. It is extremely important for manufacturers to be made aware of any problems with their products so that they may take corrective action.

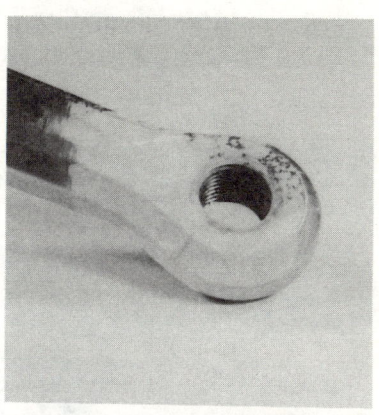
Dye Penetrant shows fine fatigue crack initiating at pedal spindle hole.

Hydrogen Embrittlement

Hydrogen embrittlement is a detrimental condition of low ductility in steels resulting from absorption of hydrogen atoms. Hydrogen can be introduced into the metal from one or more of the steps in the electroplating process. The degree of hydrogen damage is highly dependent upon the strength level of the steel. Carbon and low alloy steels, especially those with greater than 150,000 psi UTS, are subject to hydrogen damage. Details of this potential problem are discussed in the section **Plating and Anodizing** in Chapter III.

Do Frames Wear Out?
(The "Mushy Frame" Controversy)

This tricycle, conquered by corrosion, is truly worn out. (Courtesy of Michael Aisner and The Bike Race.)

When considering the purchase of a used bicycle, or selling that bike raced on last year, one wonders if the frame has somehow "worn out" or "softened". Is this a possibility, something to be concerned about? If you must have a "yes or no" answer to this general question, then the answer is No. A better answer is, "It's possible, but not likely." Professionally sponsored racers can afford the luxury of a new frame each and every year, if not more often. This only helps one to believe that frames do wear out, get soft and mushy, or something like that. A cyclist may swear that his or her frame has softened up over the past season or two. This is highly unlikely for most frames and can be explained by the rider's good imagination.

Unless at least one of the following conditions are met, the metallurgical integrity of a frameset will remain unchanged through its lifetime:

a) The frameset has been locally stressed above the yield strength (TYS) of the metal.

b) Localized stresses are attained of sufficient magnitude to cause fatigue crack initiation and growth. The critical value of stress is the metal's fatigue strength. Stresses lower than this level won't have any effect upon the metal. Fatigue problems are usually due to a design problem in the form of stress raisers.

CHAPTER II

FRAMESET MATERIALS

So, you are considering the purchase of a new bicycle, or perhaps, just a new frameset. Will it be that welded aluminum bike, that high-tech carbon fiber composite bike, or that half-steel/half-aluminum jobbie? Or is staying with the proven, reliable, and dependable Reynolds 531 steel frameset still the only way to go?

Schwinn's one-of-a-kind prototype composite bicycle, The Shadow.

At the heart of every bicycle, behind every pretty paint job, carrying that fancy component group, sporting those ultralight wheels, is the frame. Are all frames created equal? Obviously not, they range in price from one-hundred dollars for a complete bike to one-thousand dollars for just the frameset. What then, besides price and aesthetics, is the difference between frames, what should one look for, and what frame is right for me?

Until this last decade, the choice of a frame material was much more simple, simply because the choices were fewer. Steel has been the standard material used for bikes, from department store specials to the custom built frameset. Now, however, when you go shopping for a bicycle, you will encounter materials and terms that seem to come directly out of an aerospace research laboratory. Even when comparing one steel frame to another, the terminology used by each tubing or bicycle manufacturer to describe their product can be quite confusing and even misleading. *Mangaloy, Technium, chrome-moly, heat-treated, double-butted, silver* or *brass brazed, high-tension steel*. These are just some of the terms used to describe bicycle frames. *Steel, aluminum, titanium, graphite fiber composites*. You are likely to run into bicycles with framesets fabricated from each of these materials, or even a combination of them.

Money Matters

Most often, the bottom line for the consumer is cost. Even if the advantages of owning a frameset made of exotic titanium or carbon-fiber composite are significant, most of us can't make room in our budget for the eight-hundred-plus dollars needed to own just the frameset, without any components. Presently, for the cyclist wishing to keep his or her total cost for a bike under a thousand dollars, the choice is narrowed to either steel or aluminum, or a combination of the two. However, with time will come decreased production costs. This will most certainly bring the prices of more exotic frames down.

Which Frame Material is the Best?

In today's competitive and innovative bicycle market, there exist many choices when considering the purchase of a bicycle or frameset. It is logical to ask which material and construction technique is the best. Which one should I buy? The answer to this question is that there is no single correct answer. Each of the materials and processes described in this chapter and the following chapter have their own characteristics and qualities, some better, many nearly identical, and some lesser than others. Attempts have been made to generalize with statements like, "aluminum isn't a safe material for bicycle frames", or, "rigid framesets can't be made of titanium", or, "lugged frames are better than lugless frames". Blanket statements like these are not accurate and should not be made. The framebuilder's choice of materials will be based on a number of important considerations, like cost, ease of fabrication, versatility, and reliability. Often, the consumer's choice will rightly be made on the basis of personal preference or cost. If you feel you want to have an aluminum bike or must stick with a steel bike, then that is probably the right choice.

Damping Characteristics of Different Materials

Damping refers to shock and vibration absorption. For the cyclist, this means less shock and vibration that reaches the seat and handlebars. It is a well-advertised fact that aluminum has a better shock absorbency than steel. Carbon-fiber reinforced composites are credited with having even better damping characteristics than aluminum. The often-heard reasoning for this phenomenon goes something like this "Have you ever seen a bell made of aluminum?" and the obvious answer is supposed to be "No, aluminum doesn't ring like steel". Well, just what can one make of all this noise?

The property of metals that most influences vibration damping is the modulus of elasticity. Since aluminum has a modulus of elas-

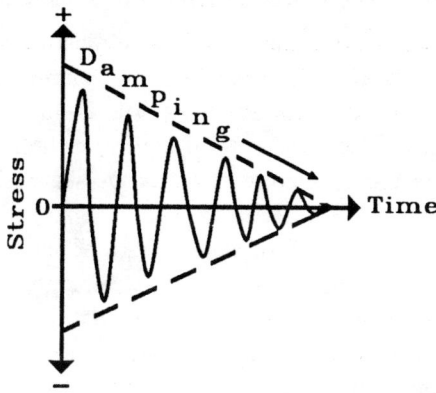

ticity 3 times less than steel, it follows that the aluminum frame would absorb and dissipate vibrations better than an identical steel frame. This is indeed true. However, there is another factor to be considered here; geometry of the system. Steel frames aren't geometrically the same as aluminum framesets. The added bulk of aluminum frames (thicker and larger diameter tubing than steel) cancels out some of the difference in vibration damping. The differences in fork materials, design, and tube joining method also contribute to differences in damping characteristics of frames. Frame size also makes a considerable difference in how a frame will absorb shock; larger frames will do a better job at dissipating vibrational stresses.

Generally, graphite fiber composites have better damping characteristics than the metals. Kevlar fibers added to the composite structure will increase this desirable effect to some extent, depending upon the relative amount of Kevlar used and the fabrication techniques used. It is generally correct to assume that a graphite fiber composite frameset will offer a more comfortable ride. Unfortunately, it would require sophisticated testing of many different actual framesets to come up with an exact quantitative answer to this matter.

The Comfort of Aluminum Frames

It is often said that aluminum frames offer a more comfortable ride because of aluminum's better shock absorbing characteristics than steel's. As mentioned in the last paragraph, this may or not be true, depending upon the type of aluminum frame construction and whether or not the frame also has an aluminum fork. The Alan and Vitus-type aluminum bikes with standard diameter tubing and aluminum forks do indeed absorb more of the road shock than the equivalent steel frame. Part of the damping effect is believed to be due to the nature of the adhesive bonded joints in the frame. However, The very rigid welded construction of Klein and Cannondale type frames with steel forks don't really offer an obvious increase in shock absorption. The additional rigidity of these frames eliminates some of the shock absorbency of aluminum frames with standard-sized tubing.

STEEL FRAMESETS

Steel is by far the most common frame material. Its technology has had a big headstart over the newer materials now used for bicycle frames. Steel is inexpensive, readily available in all shapes and sizes, and is fairly easy to work with and join together into tubular bicycle frames.

Stable of unfinished Moots Mountaineer mountain bike frames. Moots Cyclery, Steamboat Springs, Colorado.

Frame Tubing Decals

Most bicycle frames will have a decal, usually located on the seat tube just below the seat lug, which indicates the tubing used on that particular frame. Sometimes, the tubing manufacturer, the exact alloy, and its heat treated condition are indicated. Sometimes the decal gives only the tradename used for that particular tubing. Since different gauges (wall thickness) of tubing are made from the same alloy type, tubing gauge may also be indicated on the decal. By looking at the many different manufacturer's decals

on bike frames describing their steel, you would think there are perhaps fifty or more different types of steel used. However, very few varieties of steel are suitable for bicycle framesets. These decals may describe the tubing with powerful-sounding and unique words that are meant to set apart one manufacturer's product from the competition. Actually, the differences between the steel in a two-thousand dollar custom frame and in a *K-Mart special* bike are not that great. Except for the metallurgical differences discussed below, the biggest difference between steel tubes is the gauge of tubing used.

Low Carbon Steel Frames

For the lowest price bicycles, department store bikes and bikes costing not much more than a hundred dollars, the tubing used is low carbon steel. It is also often referred to as *plain carbon steel* or *high-tension steel*. Strips of this steel sheet are rolled into a tube shape and welded at the seam. Unless further treated, this welding leaves a weakened section in the vicinity of the seam. Since this steel can't achieve very high strength, the tube walls must be made quite thick and the resulting frame will be heavy.

Low carbon steel is typically fabricated into straight-gauge tubing, meaning that the wall thickness is constant throughout the length of each tube. This heavy tubing has a lot to do with why low-budget bikes ride sluggishly and lack the "liveliness" of a light weight frame. A cyclist will say that this frame gives a "harsh" ride. Though that's obviously not good for long distance riding, it's just fine for single speed cruisers and children's bicycles.

Low Alloy Steel Tubing

These are the steels used for higher-priced bicycles. Reynolds, Columbus, Tange Champion, #1 or #2, and True Temper T1 are all common examples of these steels. They are considerably more expensive than plain carbon steel tubing. However, they can be processed to higher strengths than plain carbon steel tubing and consequently, the frame weight drops considerably.

Seamless versus Welded Tubing

Whereas cheaper tubing is made from welded strip steel, the tubing in this category is most always seamless. Seamless tubing is made by piercing a hot bar of steel with a pointed tool called a mandrel and worked down into the tubular shape. This is a more expensive process than for rolled & welded tubing. The advantage of seamless tubing is that the weakened zone at the seam is eliminated.  However, welded tubing, when properly heat treated after welding, can attain the metallurgical integrity of seamless tubing. True Temper Sports, presently the only American manufacturer of high quality steel bicycle tubing, processes their welded tubing in this manner and has shown their tubing to be metallurgically and functionally equivalent to seamless tubing.

Tube Butting

This higher quality and higher strength bicycle tubing can be made quite light by a process called butting; either single, double, or even triple-butting. In his search for lighter weight bicycle tubing, Alfred M. Reynolds, of Reynolds 531 fame, invented and patented the tube butting process exactly 100 years ago, way back in 1887. By butting, the tube walls are thin in the middle and thickened at the ends where brazing or welding can cause a drop in tube strength. Also, stresses are believed to be greater near the joints, so the butting process puts more material near these joints to decrease local stresses. Taper gauge tubing, similar to butted tubing, has a tapered wall thickness throughout most or all of the tube length. However, taper gauge fork blades actually become straight gauge tubes when they are reduced in diameter towards the fork tips.

45 BICYCLE METALLURGY FOR THE CYCLIST

Note: Results of recent computer-aided stress analyses of bicycle frames have shown that the greatest stresses do not always occur in the butted section of the tubes, especially for the down tube. Some framebuilders who know this will either use heavier gauge butted tubing or straight gauge tubing for the down tube and/or seat tube on their framesets.

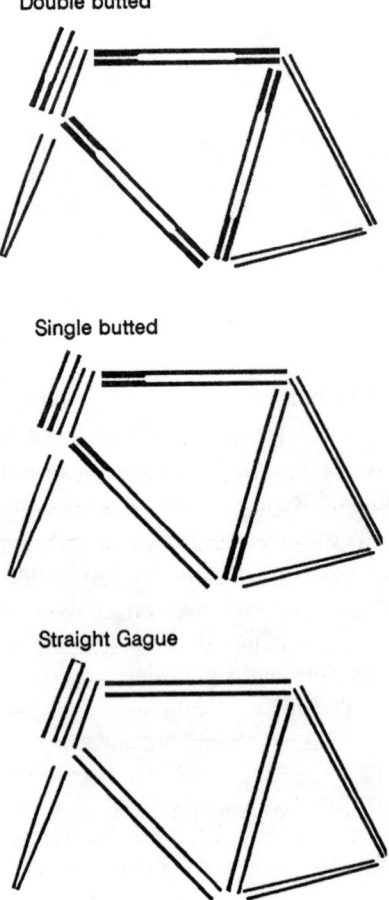

Double butted

Single butted

Straight Gague

Very High Strength Steel Tubing

The very highest strength steel bicycle tubing, namely Reynolds 753, Super Vitus 983, Tange Prestige, and Excell tubing are processed to considerably higher strengths than Reynolds 531, Columbus SL and SP, etc. As shown in the table entitled **Mechanical Properties for Steel Frame Tubing**, these four different tube materials have tensile strengths greater than 150,000 psi, at least 30% greater than Reynolds 531 or Columbus. These steels are carefully processed by a combination of heat treatment and mechanical working (drawing) to achieve their very high strengths. Contrary to popular belief, Reynolds 753 and 531 tubing have identical chemical compositions; it is the heat treatment that makes them quite different.

Super Vitus 983, though not as well known as some of the other brands, has the best metallurgical quality (mechanical properties, both before and after brazing) of all steel frame tubing. This is a bold statement that will likely be disputed by the traditionalists, but metallurgically-speaking, its charactcristics are superior. It is a chromium-vanadium-manganese-molybdenum steel that costs on the same order as both Reynolds and Columbus tubing. Because of its relatively low carbon content, brazing doesn't affect this steel's properties as much as it does the other steels. Additionally, the extremely fine grain size of this steel (the average size of crystal grains, as seen under a microscope) gives this steel excellent fatigue strength. This means that potential for fatigue failures of Vitus 983 frames become practically zero. The small amount of vanadium added to the steel promotes fine grain size. The fine grain size is easily seen in the photograph of this steel's microstructure.

Excell steel tubing has the highest strength of all steel frame tubing. This steel, a nickel-chromium steel, is quite different in composition than all of the others. Its metallurgical qualities are, like the Vitus 983, excellent. Because of the high nickel content, there is little effect on grain size from brazing temperatures. Excell tubing is used for the Masi Volumetrica frameset, racing car chassis builders, and other critical applications.

What is the advantage to using one of these very high strength steels? For one, along with the higher tensile and yield strength comes increased fatigue strength. Additionally, these tube sets can be made of lighter gauge (thinner walls) and still have the comparable load carrying capability of lower strength tubing. This means a lighter weight frame can be built without sacrificing strength.

Why isn't all high quality frame tubing made with very high strength? One reason is cost. The extra processing that it takes to achieve these mechanical properties (high strength with adequate ductility and good fatigue strength) costs more than for Reynolds 531, Columbus, and some of the others. Another important consideration is that filing, mitering, and drilling of this tubing is more difficult for the framebuilder. Additionally, the most common of these tube sets, Reynolds 753, carries a warning that the tubes are highly subject to an excessive deterioration of mechanical properties if brazing isn't performed according to strict guidelines set by T. I. Reynolds. Because of this warning, framebuilders are often fearful of brazing these new, high strength steels. Among many framebuilders, there definitely exists an attitude of keeping the status quo when it comes to frame materials. Finally, and perhaps most importantly, the availability of these tube sets to the framebuilder may not be as good as with the two "biggies", Reynolds 531 and Columbus.

An important point to consider: While the above-mentioned tubing may have higher strength, it is the elastic modulus which governs material stiffness. Elastic modulus remains essentially constant for all steels, regardless of strength. And since the wall thickness is often decreased for these tubes, the rigidity of this higher strength tubing and the resulting frameset is actually decreased. (Ultra-light weight frames of Reynolds 753 have never had a reputation for being extremely rigid.)

CHEMICAL COMPOSITION OF SOME HIGH QUALITY FRAME TUBING

Brand	%carbon	%silicon	%manganese	%molybdenum	%chromium	%nickel	%phosphorous	%sulphur	%vanadium
EXCELL	0.34	0.40	0.75	---	0.93	1.45	---	---	---
SUPER VITUS 983	0.18	0.25	1.60	0.50	0.60	---	0.025	0.025	0.16
SUPER VITUS 181 and 980	0.18	0.25	1.40	---	---	---	0.025	0.025	---
REYNOLDS 531 & 753	0.29	0.35	1.45	0.23	---	---	0.045	0.045	---
COLUMBUS SL, SP etc	0.28	0.35	0.80	0.25	1.10	---	0.035	0.035	---
ISHIWATA 015-024	0.33	0.35	0.60	0.25	1.10	---	0.035	0.035	---
TANGE CHAMPION #1, 2 3	0.30	0.23	0.48	0.16	0.84	---	0.015	0.005	---
TANGE MANGALOY 2001	0.08	0.03	2.23	---	---	---	0.015	0.070	---

MECHANICAL PROPERTIES FOR STEEL FRAME TUBING

Brand	Tensile strength lb/in^2	Yield strength lb/in^2	Elongation % in 2"	Brand	Tensile strength lb/in^2	Yield strength lb/in^2	Elongation % in 2"
EXCELL	200,100	171,000	9 min.	COLUMBUS	121,000	107,000	10
SUPER VITUS 983	156,500	128,000	18	ISHIWATA 015--024	113,200	---	5
SUPER VITUS 181 and 980	142,200	120,000	18	TANGE # 1, 2 & 3	129,500	110,000	9
REYNOLDS 753	179,200	156,800	8	TANGE MANGALOY	111,000	---	6
REYNOLDS 531	116,500	100,800	10				

Notes: SUPER VITUS has a <u>yield</u> strength of 78,250 lb/in^2 in the fully annealed state. This is 50% higher than S.A.E. 4130. The chemical composition of the steels are given as an average %. e.g. EXCELL carbon content is 0.30 to 0.38%. The information given is as advertised unless the tests results were very different. Not all steels have been tested.

Frameset Materials 50

SUPER VITUS 983

EXCELL

COLUMBUS

REYNOLDS 753

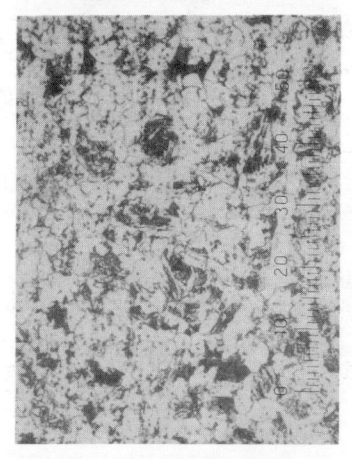
REYNOLDS 531

Reynolds versus Columbus

Over the years, there has been (and continues to be) debate over the pros and cons of tubing produced by each of these two manufacturers. Both are well known and respected by framebuilders around the world. The A. L. Columbo Iron and Steel Works has been making bicycle tubes since 1927 in Milan, Italy. Except for their cheapest tube sets, their tubing is made from chromium-molybdenum steel (Cr-Mo). T.I. Reynolds Ltd. is the English tube producer that has been manufacturing bicycle tubes since the 1890s. Though they also produce chrome-moly tubing for their Reynolds 501, 500, and 453 tube sets, their mainstay is the manganese-molybdenum (Mn-Mo) steel that goes into Reynolds 531 and 753 tube sets.

Framebuilders will have their own reasons for choosing to use one tubing or another. The mechanical properties of each steel are shown in the tables, **Chemical Composition of Some High Quality Frame Tubing** and **Mechanical Properties for Steel Frame Tubing**, found in this section. The differences between the two are not really significant. Additionally, controlled metallurgical testing has been performed by an independent researcher on Columbus and Reynolds tubing brazed with both brass and silver. The fact is that mechanical properties of each steel, in the as-brazed condition, are not different enough to say that one is definitely better than the other. In other words, each of these tube sets will make high quality bicycle frames.

Columbus SLX and SPX

This subtle new tube design from Columbus, introduced several years ago, is a structurally improved version of their SL and heavier gauge SP tubing. Five ribs, each approximately four inches long, are introduced into the four tubes that are to be brazed into the bottom bracket shell. The down and seat tube ribs are helical and chainstay ribs are longitudinal. The function of these ribs is to give greater strength and rigidity to the frame where stresses are believed to be highest. Additionally, the ribbing in the seat tube gives more strength to the region where the front derailleur hangers are brazed on. This design has been used on the Columbus steerer tubes for some time. With these ribs, the frame's total weight is increased by less than two ounces. There has been considerable promotional advertising about the advantages of SLX and SPX tubing. *Is this new design truly a significant improvement?* Some bicycle designers say that the increased bending and torsional rigidity due to the ribs is very small and is more of a marketing gimmick.

Helical ribs inside Columbus SLX steel tubing.

It is also a fact that the abrupt change from the ribbed to the non-ribbed tube section creates a stress raiser. One representative from T.I. Reynolds (the competition) indicates that there have indeed been fatigue failure problems attributable to the use of the Columbus SLX tubes. However, without unbiased results of controlled testing and evaluation, the extent or even the possibility of fatigue problems can not be exactly known.

Other Steel Tubing

There are several other steel tube producers used by bicycle manufacturers for their lineup of bikes. The more common names that one runs across are Vitus, Excell (both from France), Tange, Ishiwata, (both from Japan), and True Temper (U.S.A.). Most medium and lower priced bicycles will more likely have tubing from on of these companies. Like Columbus and Reynolds, these companies produce a range of different quality tubing for different uses. Though perhaps these manufacturers are not as well known, the characteristics of their highest quality tubing can certainly be equal to or better than the long-time standards, Reynolds and Columbus.

If there is better tubing to use than Reynolds or Columbus, why then, don't framebuilders make the switch? First, the availability and price are big considerations, and reasonably so. However, there definitely exists a reluctance towards using new products or techniques in the bicycle industry, especially when it comes to frame materials. "After all, nothing can be better than the traditional Reynold's or Columbus tubing", seems to be the attitude of many cyclists. And what is a framebuilder to do when his customers want only Reynolds or Columbus?

NONFERROUS FRAME MATERIALS

Why should there be frames of the nonferrous metals when steel has proven itself as a very good frame material? Well, for one, the search for stronger and lighter weight frame materials makes aluminum, magnesium, titanium, and composites very attractive. They all have important uses as structural materials in the aerospace industry. Lower cost and new and improved technologies are making nonferrous metals and composites the materials to watch in the bicycle industry. Another important reason why nonferrous materials are attractive is because most these metals are generally more resistant to corrosion than steel.

Aluminum Frames

Without a doubt, aluminum deserves the honor of "bicycle frame metal of the 1980s". Though the first aluminum bicycles were produced before the turn of the century, and several aluminum frames achieved commercial success in the early part of this century, it has been the efforts of several contemporary frame designers to create viable aluminum frames. And while the good majority of bicycles sold today still have steel frames, the growth of aluminum bikes has been astonishing. Today, nearly all of the large bicycle manufacturers include at least one aluminum bike in their line.

What are the major differences between the aluminum frames out on the market? The most obvious is size of tubing used. Alan and Vitus-type frames are quite similar in appearance to steel frames, using 1" and 1-1/8" diameter tubing. They use very thick-walled tubes to achieve the necessary strength and rigidity. The Cannondale, Klein, and Trek aluminum frames, however, accomplish these goals by using larger tubing, up to 1-3/4" in diameter. Though the look of these frames may take a bit of getting used to, this use of larger diameter tubing is a more efficient design for both strength and weight considerations. The one obvious drawback to using the larger diameter tubing on a frameset is decreased aerodynamic efficiency. (See the section **Frame Geometry** in Chapter III.)

Welded or Bonded Aluminum Frames

One other major difference among aluminum frames is the alloy used and method of joining. Most frames using welded construction of the alloy 6061-T6 must be re-heat treated to restore strength lost by welding. Some of the newer welded aluminum framesets are fabricated from the alloys 7005 or 7039 (or an alloy very similar in composition). These alloys, though they come from the 7XXX series known for very high strength alloys, have only slightly higher strength (20-25%) in the -T4 condition than 6061-T6. The big advantage that these alloys have going for them is strength retention after welding. 7005-T6 will retain 90-95% of its strength after welding. In general, the heat-affected zone of a weldment in a 7XXX series alloy will naturally age better than the 6XXX series alloys. This means that the post-weld heat treatment process and the tube distortion that accompanies it is eliminated.

The alternative to welding the frame tubes together is to secure them into lugs with adhesives and/or by mechanical methods. These joining methods completely eliminate exposure to high temperatures that can anneal aluminum alloys. Annealing decreases the strengthening effect of cold work or prior heat treatment. Adhesive bonding and mechanical joining of aluminum framesets is presented in Chapter III.

Anodizing of Aluminum

One neat characteristic of aluminum is its ability to form a hard, thick, protective oxide layer when chemically treated in an acid bath. This is known as anodizing. Nearly any color can be put into the anodized layer, giving the frame an attractive finish that needn't be painted. The principles of anodizing are presented at greater depth in Chapter III.

Consumer Worries

As previously mentioned, the two big hangups cyclists tend to have with aluminum frames are:

1) The fear of premature fatigue failure or a softened frame.

2) A frame that is not rigid ("stiff") enough.

Both of these concerns are addressed in terms of metallurgical principles in Chapter I. Briefly, fatigue shouldn't ever be a problem if the frame is properly designed around aluminum's fatigue life characteristics. Sufficient frame rigidity is achieved when the frame has been designed according to aluminum's modulus of elasticity.

Magnesium Frames

Until only very recently, there was no need to mention this metal for bicycle frame design. Everyone has heard of *mag* wheels, those flashy lightweight automobile wheels made of cast magnesium alloy (though many *mag* wheels are actually made of cast

The Kirk Precision cast magnesium alloy frameset.

aluminum). Well, a British aerospace and automobile design engineer, Frank Kirk, has developed and is now marketing the Kirk Precision bicycle frame.

Presently, the Kirk Precision is the only mass produced and marketed magnesium alloy frame. This frameset is a one-piece diecast structure using I-beam geometry. Though the use of I-beam shapes is very different from conventional round tubing in appearance, this shape is a very efficient use of magnesium for strength and rigidity, both bending and torsional. Due to magnesium's relatively low modulus of elasticity, the frame's weight is comparable to a light weight steel or aluminum frame. Steel and carbon fiber composite sleeves and fittings are used for component attachment. This frame has been well designed and put through extensive testing, both in the lab and out on the road.

Since the Kirk frameset is a one-piece casting, it has no need for traditional lugs that create mechanical discontinuities in the frame. Stress raiser effects are also very minimal because of this.

The casting method is a very expensive high pressure, hot chamber die-casting. By nature of this particular casting method, the metallurgical quality and geometric accuracy of this frame is controlled to very exact tolerances. This eliminates the possibility of improperly mitered, brazed, or welded joints.

One possible drawback to using some magnesium alloys is their poor corrosion resistance, generally worse than that of steel. However, this concern has been extensively tested and accounted for with the Kirk frames. The high purity of the magnesium alloy used and the high pressure casting technique both help to create a magnesium casting that has excellent corrosion resistance.

The Kirk Precision is still very new and it will take time to gain the cyclist's vote of approval and confidence. Only time will tell if Frank Kirk's innovative use of cast magnesium will catch on and become popular with the cyclist. As a final note, at the time of this book's printing, a Kirk cast magnesium alloy mountain bike frame was in the works. That shows a great deal of confidence in magnesium!

Titanium Frames

Titanium has been used very successfully in the aerospace and marine vessel industries. It is lighter than steel, but not as light as aluminum. The strength and rigidity is also between steel and aluminum. Its corrosion resistance is superior to that of steel or aluminum, and consequently, titanium frames need not be painted or anodized. The biggest drawback to titanium is the cost of raw materials, quite a bit higher than steel or aluminum. Cost of a titanium tube set is approx. $200-$300, versus $50-$100 for most steels, and often less than $50 for aluminum.

The early titanium frames produced in the 1970s, namely the Speedwell, from England, and the Teledyne Titan, from Teledyne, Inc., of the U.S., didn't achieve much commercial success. This was due to several factors; improper design, inadequate marketing, and high cost. Titanium was given a bad reputation as a frame

The world's lightest production frameset? The Speedwell titanium frameset weighs 4 lbs., 2 oz. (frame and fork, 60 cm.)

material because these frames weren't adequately designed for titanium's strength and stiffness characteristics. They were indeed very light weight, but didn't have the necessary strength and rigidity. However, with proper design, titanium frames can be fabricated that will be very competitive with the best of frames. Another idea that cyclists attach to titanium is one of notch sensitivity; that is, any scratch or stress raiser will promote catastrophic fracture. This is just too vague and general a statement. Titanium bicycle frames, when designed properly, should have no more problems with fracture than the best steel framesets. Several prototype titanium framesets show up on the bicycle trade show floors each year. The Japanese manufacturer Fuji has introduced a production welded titanium road frameset for 1987. There have even been BMX and mountain bike framesets recently fabricated from titanium in the United States. Gary Helfrich, of Fat Chance Cycles, Somerville, Mass., has a titanium mountain bike available to anyone who can afford it's approx. $2000 price.

Several knowledgeable bicycle design engineers predict a successful comeback for the titanium frameset.

COMPOSITE FRAMESETS

The expanding use of composites is certainly one of the most exciting recent technological advances in the bicycle industry. In the past ten years or so, the number of commercially available composite framesets has gone from one or two to over a dozen. What makes these materials so desirable for use in bicycle frames?

In the bicycle industry, the term *composite material* usually refers to graphite fiber/epoxy resin composites. There are many more types of composites that use other reinforcing materials and matrices, but aren't currently used for bicycles.

Credit for the first composite bike frame goes to the bicycles of wood or bamboo construction that appeared in the late 1800s. Yes, wood and bamboo are naturally occurring composite materials, though they are obviously no longer desirable for bicycles in this age of high performance.

Exxon's Graftek graphite composite frame and forkblades.

Graphite fiber composites were developed in the 1950s and first used for bicycle tubing in the early 1970s. The most familiar and only large-scale production carbon fiber bike of the 1970s was the Exxon Graftek. This frameset had a conventional diamond-shaped frame with standard diameter tubing and, surprisingly, a fork with composite fork blades. This frame was used by several big-name racers but suffered from design and construction deficiencies. It quickly fell from popularity and disappeared from the market.

Also in the early 1970s, Composite Development Corp., of San Diego, Calif., designed and constructed a bicycle of graphite fiber composite tubing. Working with Gitane, of France, CDC made a special frameset for the famous racer known for his hill climbing abilities, Lucien van Impe. Unlike the Graftek, this frameset had a conventional steel fork. Approximately only forty of these framesets were constructed by CDC. Apparently, the bicycle market was not then ready to purchase framesets of exotic materials such as graphite fiber composites.

Adhesive Bonded Tubular Frames and Molded Composite Frames:

Two fundamentally different types of graphite-fiber/epoxy-resin composite framesets can be made. At present, the more common type of frameset is the use of composite tubes put together into a conventional diamond-shaped frame. The molded composite frameset is essentially a one-piece frame that is radically different from conventional framesets. They are very new to the cycling world. The details of the different composite fabrication methods are presented in the section **Composites** in Chapter I.

As mentioned in Chapter I, all composite tubes are not created equally. They may be fabricated in very different ways with different densities, fiber-to-matrix ratios, weaving or layup patterns, etc. The resulting mechanical properties of composites are therefore widely different. Presently, the tubing with the highest strength and rigidity of all tubing manufactured for bicycles is the

ACT's graphite/epoxy composite frameset, and spool of graphite yarn, the raw material for these filament wound tubes.

100% graphite fiber (no Kevlar) filament-wound tubing; it is made by Advanced Composite Technology, Inc., of Golden, Colorado. Their complete ACT framesets have just gone through the developmental stage and will soon be available for purchase. ACT also has a composite mountain bike frameset in the works.

Carbon fiber bicycle frame development has come of age in the 1980s. There presently exist more than a dozen choices for the cyclist wishing to own a composite bicycle today. While some framesets are custom built by smaller builders, many of the big name bicycle manufacturers are putting carbon fiber bikes into their mass production lineups. Trek, Vitus, Look, Alan, Nishiki, Guerciotti, Eclipse, and Peugeot are some of the companies offering at least one carbon fiber composite bicycle with tubular construction. Almost immediately, one will find out that these framesets are not cheap. In fact, they are several-hundred dollars more expensive than most top-of-the-line steel framesets. Why then, should one purchase a bicycle with a composite frameset? Perhaps because they are very strong and rigid. Also, this tubing is highly resistant to impact and fatigue damage. Finally, however, the resulting weight of a composite frameset, as much as two pounds lighter that the steel counterpart, is possibly the most attractive feature.

One interesting variation in composite bicycle tubing is the AERORIB tubing manufactured by Quality Composites, Inc., of Riverton, Utah. This tubing has two polyimide foam ribs which are aligned along the plane of the bicycle frame in which the maximum stresses occur. This design (patent pending) saves weight by using thinner walls overall. In the plane of maximum stress, the walls are thickened by using a sandwich construction with a polyimide foam core. QCI's standard and AERORIB tubing are

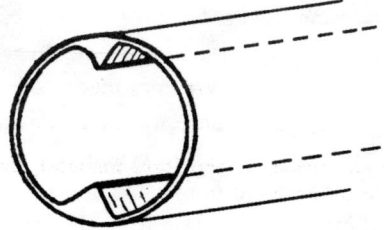

The Kestrel 4000 molded composite frameset.

rolled up on an automated rolling table from unidirectional and woven prepreg. Many different fiber/resin systems can be combined in this method to obtain maximum performance.

1987 marks the first year that a die-molded composite frameset has been mass-produced and offered for retail sale. This frame is the Kestrel 4000 Uniframe by Brent Trimble, Bevil Hogg, and Cycle Composites, Inc., of Watsonville, CA. This frame uses fabric of graphite, Kevlar, and boron fibers strategically placed to give the best use of each material. The composite is molded into an diamond-shaped frame with very aerodynamic teardrop shaped cross-section. The teardrop shape has a drag coefficient of approximately 0.4, versus the round tube's 0.9 drag coefficient. The primary drawback to frames made of a one-piece structure is the inability to fit the frame to each individual rider. In other words, these frames are not very ergonomically flexible. For a given frame size, the top tube length, chainstay length, and frame angles, are not adjustable according to each rider's build. A separate, unique mold would be necessary to fit a rider having an unusual body size. The other possible drawback to this frame is its price. The Kestrel 4000 retails for over $1,000.00. Perhaps with time, this price will drop into the range considered affordable by the masses.

COMBINATIONS OF MATERIALS

Some bicycle designers feel that a combination of different materials will give desirable characteristics to a frame. A notable example of this is the Technium line of bikes recently introduced by Raleigh of America. Though the name Technium might lead one to believe that Raleigh has discovered a new metal, these frames use a combination of common aluminum and steel alloy tubing. The three main tubes are adhesive bonded into the lugs. Seatstays and chainstays are chrome-moly steel brazed into the lugs and dropouts. Raleigh claims that by using both steel and aluminum, the desirable characteristics of each will be realized in this frame.

Antique bicycle of wood tubing clamped into aluminum lugs. Notice the wooden rims and handlebars.

Excell's CSK Tubing: Another combination of different materials is found with CSK Tubing, by Excell of France. This frame tubing consists of a very thin-walled, high strength steel tube with a graphite and Kevlar fiber-reinforced composite tube inserted within the steel tubing for added strength and rigidity. This combined tubing is light weight, very rigid, and can be brazed together with lugs, much like a conventional steel frame. The resulting frameset can also be painted and electroplated like conventional steel frames. CSK tubing is still very new and hasn't yet been picked up for large-scale use by the big bicycle manufacturers. Like all composite frame material, this tubing is presently very expensive compared to steel or aluminum. Further testing and use of this tubing will tell if it becomes a successful frame material.

Easton Aluminum's graphite fiber wrapped aluminum tubing: Easton Aluminum, of Van Nuys, California, is a manufacturer of sporting goods. They are well-known for their ski poles, tent poles, baseball bats, and archery arrow shafts. These all being tubular products, it seems logical that this company should find its way into the bicycle industry. Jim Easton, who also serves as Chairman of the Technical Committee of the United States Olympic Committee, was prompted by meetings with Ed Burke, then the Technical Director of the United States Cycling Federation, to pursue bicycle applications for their very successful technology used to produce strong, rigid, and reliable arrow shafts. Presently, Easton is working on a graphite/epoxy wrapped core of very high strength aluminum tubing. They are working to make bicycle frame tubing that will capitalize on the desirable properties of both graphite composites and aluminum. Of course this tubing will necessarily be adhesive bonded, not welded or brazed. Easton feels that this is a superior way to assemble frame tubing, anyway. The U.S. Team's 1988 Olympic bicycles may show up to the starting lines exhibiting this technology.

Miyata Carbon Tech 5000: This new frameset, introduced in 1987 by Miyata is a creative combination of carbon fiber composites and metal wire. This proprietary process uses a very fine

50 micron diameter wire wrapped around the outside of the three carbon fiber main tubes. The wire, advertised as *amorphous*, is said to have a non-aligned crystalline structure to it. However, amorphous, by definition means "not having a crystalline structure". Use of the word *amorphous* is a misnomer. In any case, this very high strength wire is wrapped tighter near the lugs than in the middle of the tubes to create an effect similar to butted steel tubing. Is this really a revolutionary design that is structurally superior to other composite frame designs? Only thorough road and laboratory testing performed on these framesets can properly answer that question.

Donavan Ultraperformance Bicycles' aluminum reinforced steel tubing: Ken Janke, custom framebuilder of Boulder, Colorado, uses a 1/8" thick 6061-T6 aluminum strut that runs through the diameter of the ends of the frame's three main tubes. These struts allow Ken to use a thinner gauge steel tubing and still maintain adequate strength and rigidity. A 26 lb. steel mountain bike is created with this design. The aluminum 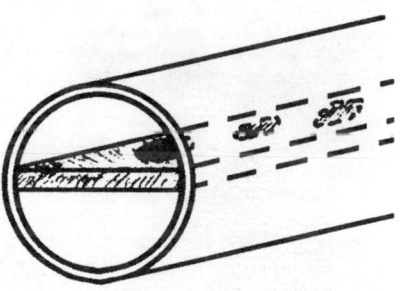 strut is press fit into the steel tubing; no brazing or adhesives are used. This lessens any potential stress raiser effect that a bonded strut would create. The struts are drilled for minimizing weight.

FRAME GEOMETRY

Besides the choice of materials, much of what characterizes a bike frame is its geometry. Some important geometric variables are: angular relationships between frame tubes (frame angles), diameter of tubing, shape of tubing, wall thickness of tubes. Quantifying the effects of variations in frame angles is quite complex and beyond the scope of this book. It has been noted elsewhere in this book that strength and rigidity increase as tube diameter and/or wall thickness increase.

One interesting geometric aspect of frame design is the use of tube shapes other than round. This can be as subtle as dented or ovalized chainstays, or very obvious variations such as diamond-shaped tubing (as found on the Picchio, the new Rossin, and Colnago Master frames) and teardrop-shaped tubing, and even star-shaped tubing.

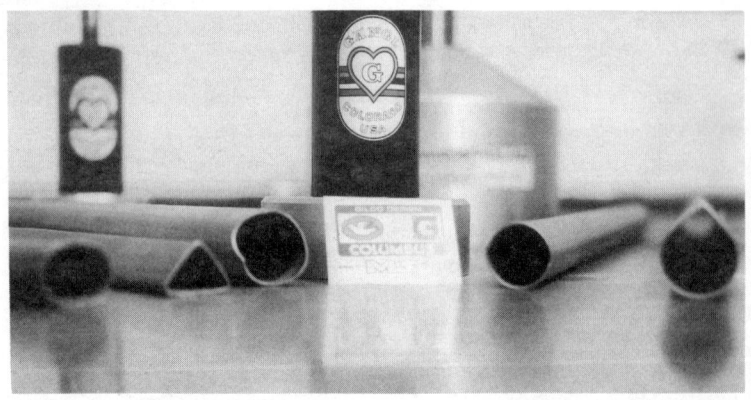

Columbus MS (Multi-Shape) tube set.

Columbus, in collaboration with Gilco Design, an Italian design firm, has introduced their MS (Multi-Shaped) tubeset. This is a complete bicycle tubeset made from their chrome-moly steel with quite a few unique geometric features for each different tube. Their stress analyses on framesets has led them to design each tube with a different profile, according to the loading each tube will experience when ridden. Of course, specially shaped lugs are also included with this tube set. Also found on some custom frames are smaller double tubes for either the seat tube (as with the Rigi, of Italy) or down tube (Donavan Cycles' mountain bike frames).

From the standpoint of combined weight and rigidity considerations, a single round tube is the most efficient use of material.

The Donavan Outback 2+2, sporting a double down tube for increased strength and rigidity with a minimal weight increase.

However, other considerations, such as increased aerodynamic efficiency, increased rigidity in one particular direction, wheel clearance, or component fitting, must also be taken into account. Teardrop-shaped tubing has increased rigidity in one direction, and is certainly 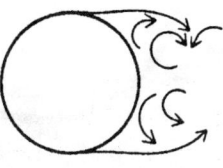 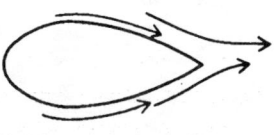 more aerodynamic, but suffers a lack of rigidity in the perpendicular direction. Crimped or diamond-shaped tubing does give increased rigidity due to the structural effects of angles and corners. However, this tubing is more expensive to manufacture and is not as easy for the framebuilder to work with as round tubes are. Double tubes gives increased rigidity but at the expense of greater weight. Many of these variations are a novelty and not much more. This is why these variations aren't more widely agreed upon and implemented by other manufacturers and framebuilders.

There are two basic ways to make bicycle frame tubing more rigid:

1) Increase the wall thickness of the tubing.

2) Increase the diameter of the tubing.

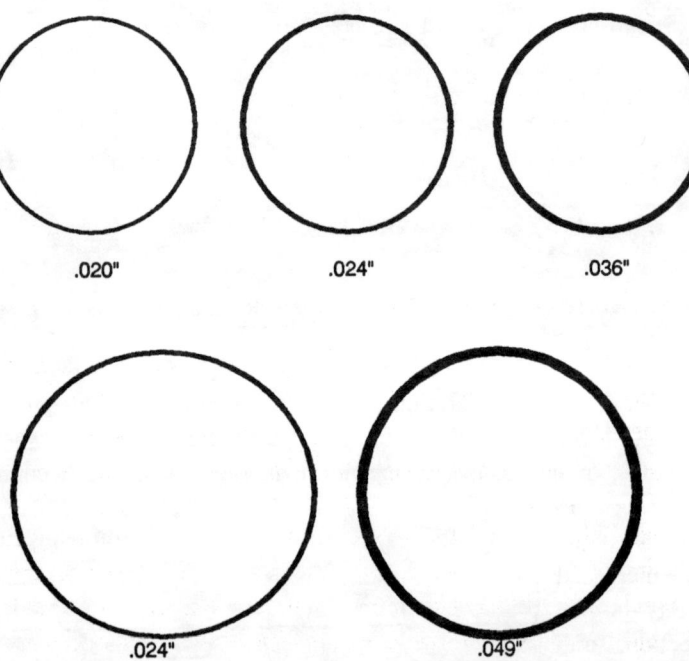

The best method, and the solution used by Klein, Trek, Cannondale, and others, is a combination of both thicker-walled and larger diameter tubing. In 1985, Gary Klein received a patent on his "Power Tubing" method of using larger diameter nonferrous tubing for frame construction. Many of the composite frames out on the market also make use of thicker and larger diameter tubing for adequate rigidity and strength. As mentioned earlier, the one obvious drawback to using larger diameter tubing is the decreased aerodynamic efficiency.

CHAPTER III

BICYCLE FRAME CONSTRUCTION

LUGS, BRAZING, AND WELDING

The way in which the tubes are put together is critical to producing a quality frameset. Steel tubing may always be joined by either brazing or welding. However, with other frame materials, the choice of joining method is often limited by the type of alloy used. For example, the popular standard diameter aluminum framesets (Vitus, Alan, etc.) use aerospace epoxy adhesives to join the tubing to the lugs. Welding this tubing would severely weaken the aluminum. Other aluminum framesets (Klein, Cannondale, etc.) weld the aluminum together and then heat treat the frame to restore full strength to the tubes. Some aluminum tubing can't be easily welded and must be bonded with an adhesive. This is the case for frames made with True Temper T2, their high strength aluminum tubing.

Lugs and Dropouts

The lugs used on conventional steel frames are also made of steel, either stamped and welded or cast. Though precision investment cast lugs are preferred by most framebuilders for high-end

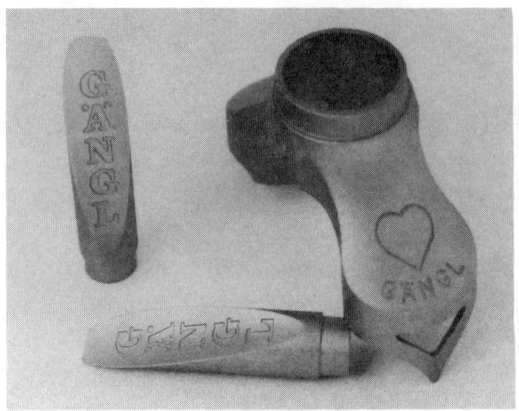

Custom cast fork crown and seatstay caps.

bikes, stamped and welded lugs (stamped from steel sheet, formed into shape, and welded at the seams) aren't especially a sign of cheap or inferior construction. Some framebuilders prefer stamped and welded lugs because they have more ductility than cast lugs, so they may be bent to make different size frames with different frame angles.

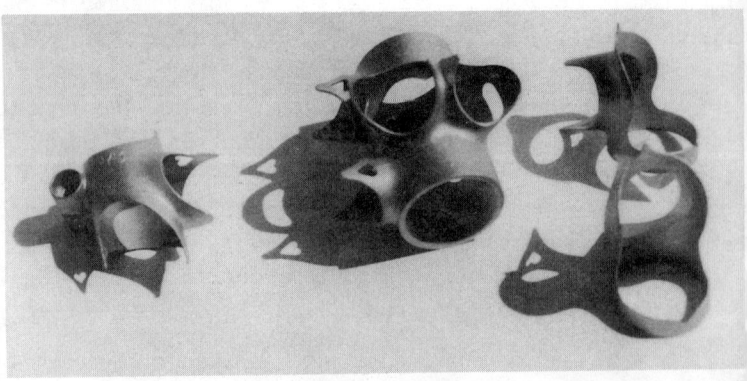

Custom investment cast lugs. Courtesy of Gängl Custom Cycles.

Dropouts, both front and rear, are either stamped, cast, or forged from steel. Stamped dropouts will be found on the most inexpensive bicycles. Forged dropouts are standard on most steel bikes costing over two-hundred dollars and are metallurgically superior (stronger) than stamped dropouts.

Lugless Construction: Welded or Fillet Brazed

It was previously thought that for a frame to be of any quality, it must have lugged construction. In the lower price range, lugged frames may be better than lugless frames, but there are many high quality bicycles out on the market now, especially mountain bikes, that are either welded or fillet brazed without lugs. Fillet brazing is a direct brazing of one tube to another, without the use of lugs. Brass filler metal is built up around the joints for strength and aesthetics.

Welding, a higher temperature process than brazing, actually melts one tube into another with filler metal. The success of welded BMX and mountain bike frames has proven that lugs aren't a necessary requirement for a frame to be strong and durable. However, some cyclists prefer the artistic looks of brazed lugs to the relatively unattractive welded joints.

Lugless fillet brazed bottom bracket shell. Courtesy of Gängl Custom Cycles.

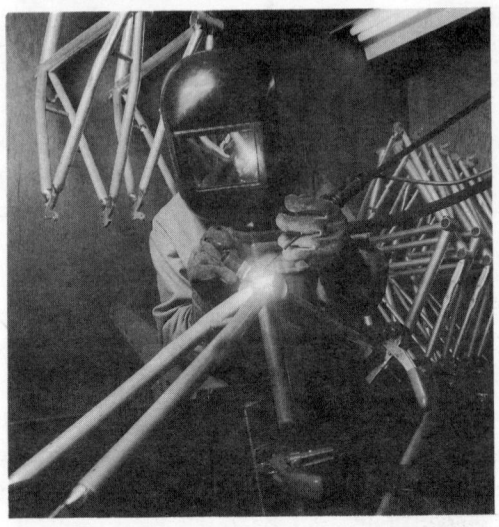

TIG welding the Cannondale aluminum frameset.

Internal Lugs

There is an increasing use of internal lugs by steel framebuilders and manufacturers. These lugs fit inside the tubes as opposed to the conventional lugs that slide over the tubing. Internal lugs are usually seen on adhesive bonded aluminum and composite framesets. Since the tubing fits over the lug instead of inside it, internal lugs can allow for the use of slightly larger diameter tubing, thereby increasing frame rigidity. Masi, of Italy, one of the world's most respected framebuilders, uses this technique for their Volumetrica frameset. Nishiki has also recently made use of this construction method in their top of the line bikes.

Brass or Silver Brazing?

For those steel frames that are lugged and brazed, the choice is made by the builder whether to use brass or silver for the brazing filler metal. (There is no bronze braze metal used by framebuilders. This word is incorrectly used when referring to brass.) There is a whole spectrum of brasses that can be used for brazing filler metal, each with a different melting range.

The biggest difference between the two brazing choices, either silver or brass, is the temperature at which the braze alloys liquidify and flow. This is important when discussing the effects of brazing upon the metallurgical integrity of the steel tubing. Why? Because there is a critical temperature at which steel alloys will change their microscopic crystal structure. This temperature is approximately 1340° F.

- **Silver brazing**: These alloys flow at temperatures well below 1340° F. Consequently, if the temperature is kept below 1340° F, the only thing that can happen to the steel is for it to be tempered (softened). It has been shown that the softening that does occur may reduce the steel's strength by as much as 20%. However, this is not a drastic drop. The tubing will still perform as intended if designed properly.
- **Brass brazing**: The brasses flow at temperatures above steel's upper critical temperature. Therefore, the concern becomes focused on the rate at which the steel cools from this temperature. Slow cooling will cause the steel to be normalized. This translates to lower strength and higher ductility. The normalized condition is what is found in standard Reynolds 531, Columbus, and most other chrome-moly tubing. Very rapid cooling, or "quenching", can increased the strength of the steel, but at the expense of decreased ductility.

An additional important consideration for the above discussion is the metallurgical condition of the tubing before brazing. The steel can either be in the normalized condition (Reynolds 531, or Columbus), or the quenched and tempered condition (Reynolds 753 and Tange Prestige). Reynolds insists on silver brazing their 753 tubing to avoid eliminating the original quenched and tempered condition.

There has been limited independent research published on the relative effects of brass and silver brazing on steel. Very briefly, the most important conclusion of controlled research is that neither brazing method is "bad" or especially worse than the other. A framebuilder may have a particular reason for using either brass, silver, or both. There are legitimate pros and cons for the use of each; most have to do with ease of brazing. One thing for certain is that it is incorrect to make the broad statement that either brass or silver makes a better, stronger frame joint for all joint configurations.

Cast Bicycle Frames

How convenient it would be if one could simply pour molten metal into a bicycle mold, let it cool, and take it out and ride it! This may sound far-fetched but this is roughly how the cast magnesium alloy frames by Kirk Precision Ltd. are fabricated. By casting a bicycle frame, use of tubes, lugs, filing, brazing, welding, nega-

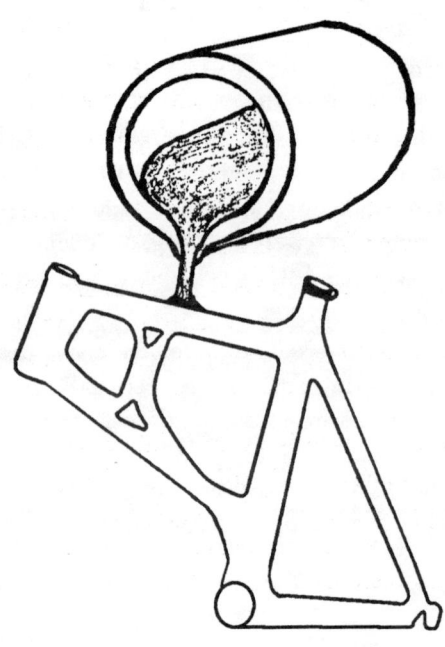

tive effects of heat, and frame alignment are all unnecessary and are eliminated. (See **Magnesium Frames**, Chapter II). However, only magnesium and possibly aluminum are light weight enough (have low enough densities) to cast into a bicycle frame. A cast steel frameset would probably weigh 25 pounds!

ADHESIVE BONDING and MECHANICAL JOINING

Adhesive bonding is a method of joining that relies on the bond formed between the chemical adhesive and the metal. This is the standard method for joining aluminum and composite frame tubes that cannot be welded or brazed. In the past, there have been joint failures due to de-bonding and separation of the tubes from the lugs. Fortunately, adhesive bonding technology and process control has advanced to where this is not a common problem for framesets built today. Adhesive bonding offers the following potential advantages:

- Joints can be made at lower temperatures, thus eliminating the metallurgical effects of brazing or welding.
- The process can be cheaper because of the lower power requirements and consumable costs (adhesive vs. brazing rods & fluxes.)
- The adhesive bonding process can allow for improved strength-to-weight ratios for the frameset.

The most common of the non-welded aluminum frames, the Vitus Duralinox 979 frame, is adhesive bonded using a shallow conical taper that is pressed into cast aluminum lugs. The large surface area of the tapered joint assures adequate joint strength.

Mechanical joining is primarily used for attaching some of the smaller fixtures to a frameset. Riveting, press-fitting, expansion joints, bolting, or screwing are all common mechanical joining methods. The French bicycle manufacturer Peugeot has very recently introduced an aluminum frameset that relies on mechanical joining of the tubes rather than welding or adhesive bonding.

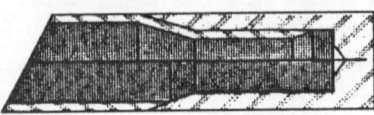

Peugeot has collaborated with Cegedur/ Pechiney, also of France, to use aerospace technology in creating this frameset. In the same way that the wings of France's famous Airbus airliner are joined to the fuselage, this bicycle's tubing is locked to the lugs mechanically.

A combination of mechanical joining and adhesive bonding is known as the "screw and glue" process and has been used on some of the standard diameter aluminum bicycles. The most notable example is the Alan, created in the mid-1960s by the Italian engineer, Mr. Falconi, and marketed by Gitane for several years. Joint strength and integrity is achieved by utilizing both a threaded connection and an adhesive bond. Kettler, of West Germany, presently produces an aluminum frameset that uses both adhesives and expansion-joint inserts for joining their tubing.

PLATING and ANODIZING

Chrome Plating

This process of depositing a thin coating of chromium over a steel frame or fork produces this attractive and very durable scratch resistant finish. Other metals can be plated onto steel the way that chrome is. However, with the exception of perhaps nickel, their appearance and durability is not on the level of chrome plating.

Hydrogen Embrittlement from the Plating Process?

Problems can arise from the plating process if precautions are not taken. One potential problem is called hydrogen embrittlement. During the plating, hydrogen atoms may enter the steel and embrittle it if conditions are right. Embrittlement will cause severe cracking in the steel. The degree of hydrogen damage is highly dependent upon the strength level of the steel. The higher the tensile strength, the greater is the hydrogen embrittlement susceptibility. The plain carbon and low alloy steels with greater than 150,000 psi UTS are subject to hydrogen damage. The frequency of occurrences of this phenomenon in the bicycle tubing is rare and not well understood. Whether or not there are many problems of hydrogen-embrittled bicycle frame tubing is not well documented. In any case, this concern should not be ignored by framebuilders and platers. Immediate baking at approximately 350° F will ensure that no hydrogen stays trapped within the steel. The hydrogen will diffuse out of the steel at this elevated temperature.

Acid Attack

The other potential danger of metal plating may arise when frame tubes are immersed in an acid bath to clean the steel before plating. If this acid enters the inside of the tubing through the tube ends or brazing vent holes and is not rinsed out, the small amounts of acid left in the tube can cause accelerated corrosion of the steel. Over time, the strength of the tubing may become jeopardized from tube wall thinning. Rinsing the frame or fork in an alkaline bath (baking soda, for example) will neutralize the acid so that accelerated corrosion will not occur.

Plugging vent holes, rinsing the frame tubing in a neutralizing solution after pickling and plating, and baking the fork or frame after plating, will prevent any possible problems. For mass produced, store-bought bikes, it must be assumed that the manufacturer was aware of potential problems with chrome plating and took necessary precautions. For the customer having a custom bike built and chromed, he or she should be certain that the builder takes these precautions against possible complications associated with the plating process.

Does Chrome Plating Reduce the Fatigue Life of Steel?

Since bicycles are subject to repeated stresses that may, in some instances, cause fatigue failures, nothing should be done to framesets that will significantly decrease their fatigue resistance. It has been shown that chrome plating may reduce the fatigue strength of some steels, though these tests weren't conducted on bicycle frames or tubing. There has been no published research done on the effect that chrome plating has on actual bicycle frames.

One thing for certain, there are many bicycles, both road and mountain bikes with entirely chrome plated frames, which have been ridden for years without fatigue problems. From this standpoint, one would have to conclude that chrome plating does not significantly effect the fatigue life of bicycles frames.

At least one prominent frame builder refuses to chrome plate his forks because of his belief that "the plating decreases the elasticity of the fork". This argument has very little scientific basis for it. Elasticity is determined by the elastic modulus of the system and the very thin layer of plating over the bulk of steel has only a minor effect upon the fork's rigidity. Think about this: many springs are chrome plated and retain their elasticity quite well.

Aluminum Anodizing

Aluminum has a natural tendency to form an oxide coating upon its surface. Metal oxides are simple chemical compounds of the metal plus oxygen. Anodizing is an electrochemical process that enables this oxide film to grow and be thickened by a factor of more than a thousand. Anodizing is accomplished by immersing the part into an acid bath and applying an electric current through the part and bath. Unlike painting or chrome plating, the anodized layer is actually part of the aluminum and can't be stripped-off or flake-off like chrome or paint. Different combinations of acid baths, temperatures, and electric current densities can produce various anodized surfaces. Hard anodizing is a special type of anodizing done in an acid bath at low temperatures (20° to 40° F). The end result is a thicker and harder oxide layer. Coloring of anodized layers can be achieved by the use of organic dyes or varying the conditions of the anodizing process.

Anodizing Is Not A Heat Treatment

It should be stressed that anodizing is purely a surface treatment. It has no effect upon the bulk aluminum underneath the anodized layer. Misleading advertising by sales representatives for various bicycle rim manufacturers has contributed to the erroneous belief that anodizing is a form of heat treatment.

CHAPTER IV

BICYCLE COMPONENTS

Unlike the many choices available for frameset materials, there really are not many different material choices for the other components. For most metallic components of a bicycle, aluminum is the material of choice. Aluminum is light weight, has good corrosion resistance, is easy to fabricate, and usually has adequate mechanical properties. For parts requiring mechanical properties that aluminum can't offer, steel must be used. For example,

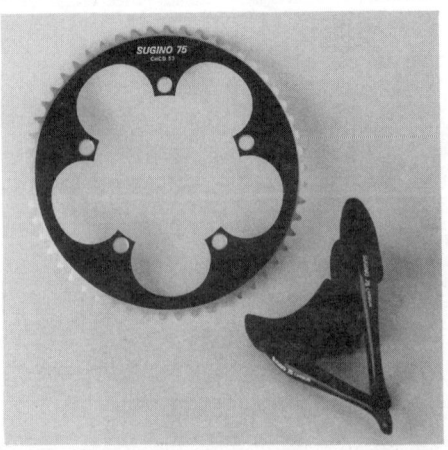

Graphite composite brake levers and reinforced chainring, by Sugino.

springs must be made of special spring steel. There are also many highly stressed small parts (bolts, nuts, etc.) that require the high strength of steel. Bearings and bearing races must be made of high carbon steel or stainless steel for high hardness and excellent wear resistance. In many instances, the small weight savings achieved by substituting titanium, aluminum, or magnesium for steel is just not worth the bother or increased cost.

RIMS and SPOKES

Rims

Except for rims found on very inexpensive bikes, today's bicycle rims are almost always made from aluminum alloys. Aluminum's excellent strength-to-weight ratio and good formability make it the

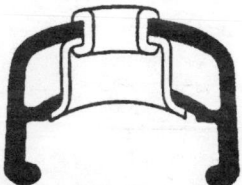 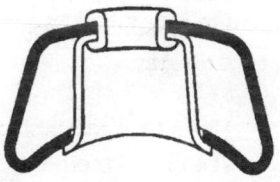

material of choice for wheel rims. Aluminum rims are now made as cheap and as strong as steel rims. So, there is little apparent reason for using steel rims on most bicycles. If one searches hard enough, he or she will be able to find rims fabricated from titanium or nature's composite, wood. However, they are a novelty and usually offer no advantage over aluminum rims. Carbon fiber rims are produced, but carry a very high price tag on them; and they must be used with special brake pads that will not damage the rim's braking surfaces. Titanium rims are presently manufactured by Araya, of Japan, for track racing. These rims are a bit heavier than their aluminum counterparts, but are stronger and more rigid. Fiamme, of Italy, also makes a titanium bicycle rim for tubular tires.

There are many mysteries and rumors floating around in the cycling world about bicycle rims. This is largely due to the fierce competition that exists between rim manufacturers. The fact that a rim is heat treated and/or hard anodized is often used as a selling point. Today, the dark gray or black anodized finish is so popular that it is difficult to sell rims with polished or clear anodized finishes. *Are anodized and/or heat treated rims superior to the others?*

First of all, whether a rim is truly heat treated or not depends upon the particular aluminum alloy chosen. The alloy must belong to either the 2XXX, 6XXX, or 7XXX series in order to be heat treated. There are three ways to increase the strength of aluminum alloy rims:

1) Strengthen by increased amounts of cold work from the extrusion process. Most aluminum rims are formed by extruding, which cold works the metal to higher strengths.

2) Use a heat treatable alloy and heat treat the rim to the -T4 or -T6 temper.

3) Use more metal and/or change the rim's cross-section shape.

Method 1) is how most rims get their strength. As for the second method, a truly heat treatable alloy must be used. The added heat treatment step increases the cost to produce the rim. The surest method of producing a very strong and rigid rim is to used Method 3). Rigidity is a function of the rim's geometric design (the amount of metal and its placement). However, more metal means greater weight, which is an undesirable feature of rims. Most rims that have a reputation for their excellent durability are approximately 100 grams (about 4 ounces) heavier than the very lightest weight rims. This is largely the reason for the success of the famous Mavic SSC hard anodized rims.

Some of the rim manufacturers that presently produce heat treated rims are: Matrix rims (Tru-America Corp.), Campagnolo, Rigida, Wolber, and Mistral (Sun Metal Products, Inc.). Not all models from every one of these producers are heat-treated, however.

When the first of the dark gray and black anodized rims hit the market, many cyclists thought that this was an indication of extra-strong heat treated rims. After all, it does seems reasonable that this dark coloration would be a consequence of the heat treatment process. However, it is now well understood that anodizing has absolutely nothing to do with heat treatment and that the color of the rim has nothing to do with whether the rim is or is not heat treated. It is certainly possible for bicycle rims to be both anodized and heat treated. Many rims are made this way.

Are anodized rims stronger more rigid than non-anodized rims? Well, it has been shown that the anodized layer does increase the bending rigidity of a rim by approximately 20%. However, this certainly doesn't mean that the built wheel will be that much more strong or rigid. In fact, the increase in total wheel rigidity will be on the order of only 1%. The primary function of anodizing is for increased wear resistance and corrosion resistance.

Spokes and Nipples

Bicycle spokes are exposed to many severe loading and unloading cycles and to extremely corrosive conditions. Therefore, spokes are most often fabricated from plated plain-carbon steel or from stainless steel. Those spokes that are referred to as *zinc spokes* are actually a plain carbon steel with zinc plating for corrosion resistance. Titanium spokes have been made but don't have the very high strength and stiffness needed. Also, they aren't generally considered to be worth their high cost.

One could compare tensile strength and other mechanical properties of different brands of spokes, but there is much more to strong, reliable, and high quality spokes than simply their mechanical properties. Most spokes breakage occurs as a result of fatigue. There are many aspects of spoke design other than the steel's tensile strength that affect the resulting fatigue life of a spoke.

Wheelsmith Fabrications, Inc., an American-based manufacturer of spokes and wheels, have conducted extensive studies on the design characteristics of spokes. They have demonstrated that proper geometric design and control over spoke fabrication is critical to spoke quality. Based on conclusions from their research on spokes and bicycle wheels, here are some specifications for the spokes which they produce:

- Use of an ultra-high grade of stainless steel that has been carefully progressively drawn and annealed to fine gauge wire.
- Carefully monitored drawing processes to give a good surface finish with a minimum of microscopic surface flaws.
- Carefully designed and fabricated spoke head elbow radius.
- Rolled threads instead of cut threads. Rolling realigns rather than interrupts the grain structure of the metal. The stress raiser effect of the threads is minimized by rolling.

Spoke nipples are usually made from brass that has been plated with nickel. The nipples produced by Wheelsmith Inc. are plated with Duristan, a more durable and more corrosion resistant metal plating. Anodized aluminum nipples are available for the extreme weight conscious cyclist. A weight savings of only 24 grams, or approx. 1 ounce, is realized by using aluminum nipples.

HANDLEBARS, FREEWHEELS, CHAINS, ETC.

Aluminum and Magnesium Alloy Freewheels

There is a lot of metal that goes into freewheels. A steel freewheel weighs about a pound. Considerable weight savings are achieved by substituting aluminum or magnesium for steel. Both aluminum and magnesium freewheels are produced and are available for a hefty price. Some designs incorporate these lighter alloys into both body and cogs, and some designs use the lighter cogs on a steel body. The lightest freewheel manufactured is the Maillard 700 freewheel, using the magnesium alloy AZ31 for both the body and cogs. The Campagnolo aluminum freewheel is the most popular of the lightweight freewheels. You can be assured that when Campagnolo puts one of these light freewheels out on the market, the design characteristics have been thoroughly investigated and optimized. Nevertheless, aluminum and magnesium alloys lack the hardness and wear resistance of high strength steel, and consequently, these freewheels don't wear as well as steel freewheels.

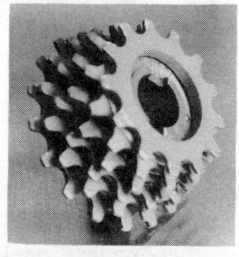

Maillard magnesium alloy freewheel, perhaps the world's lightest.

Titanium Components

Several bicycle component manufacturers, including Campagnolo, have made or still make titanium components. Though titanium isn't as light as aluminum, it can be used to replace steel axles, spindles, and the like, where aluminum absolutely can't hold up to the high stresses. The two advantages of substituting titanium for steel are weight savings and corrosion resistance. Bulky, highly stressed components that are usually made of steel are fabricated from the titanium alloy Ti-6Al-4V. The two advantages of substituting titanium for steel are weight savings and better corrosion resistance. A weight savings of approximately 40% is realized by using titanium instead of steel for the same part. For a bottom bracket spindle, this means three to four ounces.

The drawbacks of using titanium for these parts are decreased strength and stiffness, and much higher cost. Titanium has only 2/3 the stiffness of steel, and since the part can't be beefed up by using more titanium, these spindles and axles have a tendency to bend and/or break, especially when used by the stronger and heavier riders. In other words, the safety factor is significantly decreased when titanium is used where steel normally would be used. This combined with the cost, three to five times the price of a steel unit, has kept the use of titanium parts from popularity.

Campagnolo's original Super Record titanium bottom bracket spindle was hollow with threaded bolt holes, like typical steel spindles. However, this design was not rigid enough and the newer style of a solid spindle using a threaded end and nuts was created to alleviate this problem. Though this design is better, reports of spindle failures have still continued.

Titanium Chains

Titanium chains are rare but have been offered for retail sale by Regina of Italy. The entire chain cannot be made of titanium, however. The necessary use of steel for pins, rollers, and bushings puts the weight of this chain up near that for a steel chain. Apparently, the high cost of this item is just not worth the weight savings.

Handlebars

Except for mountain bikes, nearly all better quality bicycle handlebars are made from extruded aluminum, usually a 5XXX series alloy. One large manufacturer, 3ttt (techno-tubo-torino) of

Italy, uses the stronger heat treatable alloys for their handlebars. Their top- of-the-line bars, the "SL" model, uses the very high strength 7075-T6 alloy in order to make a lighter yet stronger handlebar.

Note: Drilling of handlebars for brake cable routing is not advisable. The stress raiser effect of the hole can lead to catastrophic failure of the bars. See the section **Stress Raisers in Failure of Metals**, Chapter I.

Magnesium or Aluminum Alloy Saddle Rails

Several saddle manufacturers substitute either magnesium or aluminum in place of the standard steel rails. Though the weight savings here is significant, these rails experience repeated tensile stresses large enough to cause fatigue problems. Fatigue cracks commonly grow until the saddle rails break catastrophically, leaving the cyclist without a comfortable place to sit! This is one example of light metal substitution that creates a marginal design safety factor. The weight savings just isn't worth it if a ride is ended prematurely due to a broken saddle.

CHAPTER V

FUTURE DIRECTIONS

After realizing all of the materials technology present in today's bicycle industry, one must wonder, "What next?" Are metals dying as structural materials? Will they be entirely replaced by the

The experimental composite bicycle by Paolo Martin and 3ttt.

new breed of composite materials? The answer to the last two questions is, "Not likely." Though the use of alternative materials are presently on the increase, there are many applications for which metals can't be replaced.

What motivates bicycle development? One very big motivational factor has always been simply the desire to go faster and further. This means higher performance and lighter weight materials must be sought. The current craze of bicycle racing that began in the late 1970s has put pressure on builders and designers to improve their products. Manufacturers must keep up with increased consumer awareness and expectations by producing better products from better materials.

Presently, we in the Eighties are in a very dynamic revolutionary developmental period for bicycle materials. In the past few years, aluminum has gone from being considered as an exotic frame material to a standard of the industry. Composites have risen from their status as an exotic, mysterious, and very unaffordable frame material to a reasonable choice of materials for high-end bicycles. Where does this all lead to? What new metals and other materials are waiting for cyclists just over the horizon?

Though it may sound dramatic, it appears that our world is presently moving into a new age of technology: *The Engineered Materials Age*. Metallurgy, which was the forerunner of Materials Science, is slowly becoming engulfed by it. It no longer makes sense to segregate metals from other materials, since the benefits of each must be weighed in the design process. Conventional metals are likely to become less competitive as users demand reduced weight, better performance, increased reliability, and lower costs. What metals, ceramics, and polymers cannot do alone, they can probably do together, in composites engineered to achieve precisely the performance characteristics needed for major advances in engineered products, including the bicycle. The following diagram illustrates the interaction between metals, polymers (plastics, resins, composite fibers, etc.) and ceramics:

91 BICYCLE METALLURGY FOR THE CYCLIST

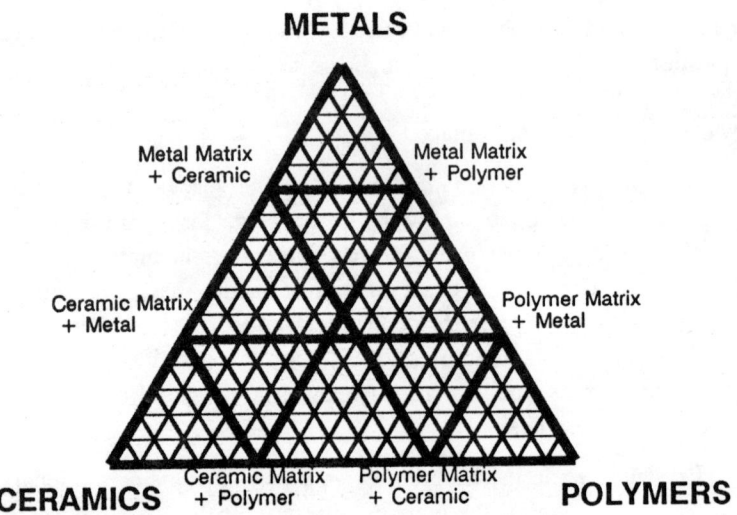

As previously mentioned in this book's introduction, today's "high-tech" bicycle most likely has roots in the aerospace and/or automotive industries. Here is a quote from the editor of *Materials Engineering*, a periodical devoted to new developments in the field of metallurgy and materials science. These are the opening lines to an article entitled "Materials in Aerospace":

"Developments in materials for space vehicles and advanced aircraft point the way to the less exotic applications of tomorrow. If the current level of activity is any indication, non-aerospace materials users have a lot to look forward to."

There are three notable aerospace programs presently underway that are relying heavily on new materials: The Transatmospheric Vehicle (TAV), the Advanced Tactical Fighter (ATF), and the Manned Space Station. Not all new aerospace materials and process technology will be transferable to the bicycle industry, of course. However, the future does sound quite promising to bicycle designers in a number of developments. What follows is a rundown of new materials and processes that show good potential for use in the bicycle industry, and in some cases, are already being used by bicycle designers to make next year's superbikes:

Metal Matrix Composites: Called MMC for short, these structural materials are similar to graphite-epoxy composites, but use metal instead of epoxy for the matrix.

Tubing of graphite fiber-reinforced 6061-T6 aluminum is presently being used for critical aerospace applications. It is very strong and lightweight. Presently, the drawback is this material's cost. Right now, it is too expensive for use as a bicycle frame material. Give this material a few years in the aerospace industry to drop the cost and develop fabrication processes. (Remember the cost and complexity of the first calculators, digital watches, CD players, etc.)

Another promising MMC is the new family of silicon carbide (Si-C) reinforced metals, most notably, aluminum and magnesium. Silicon carbide, in the form of particulates, discontinuous fibers, or continuous fibers, is dispersed throughout the metal matrix in order to significantly strengthen and stiffen it. True Temper Sports, the U.S. manufacturer of steel and aluminum bicycle tubing, golf club shafts, etc., has recently revealed that they have already built two secret prototype bicycle frames fabricated from Si-C reinforced aluminum! The cost of this material is reasonable, too; not much more than twice the cost of conventional aluminum alloys.

Boron reinforced titanium alloys are yet another promising MMC that may soon find its way into bicycle design. Like graphite, boron is a very high strength fiber material.

Aluminum-Lithium Alloys: This new series of aluminum alloys uses additions of the element lithium (chemical symbol Li) to make alloys that are lighter weight, stronger, and stiffer than the existing aluminum alloys. Lithium is the lightest metal known to mankind and is too volatile to be used by itself for structures. This development has just gotten past the experimental stage, and these alloys are already being incorporated into airplane and spacecraft design. A very recent overview of the materials technology for the aerospace industry stated that Al-Li alloys appear to be the aerospace metal of the future. That's a pretty good indication that these alloys have excellent potential. The cost of Al-Li alloys? Good news; not much more than traditional high strength aluminum alloys.

Magnesium Alloys: Bicycle designers have stayed away from magnesium because of its low stiffness, having approximately only one-half of aluminum's stiffness. A conventional frameset would just not be rigid or strong enough. However, Frank Kirk, an English aerospace designer, has developed a cast magnesium alloy frameset that has the riding characteristics very similar to that of a high quality conventional steel or aluminum frameset. Second generation magnesium frames may use magnesium metal matrix composites. The Dow Chemical Company is doing extensive research and development of silicon carbide and aluminum oxide reinforced magnesium. Results of their work look quite promising, both from an engineering standpoint and an economical standpoint.

Titanium Alloys: The titanium alloys have been used in the bicycle industry for over ten years now with limited commercial success. Problems with early design and fabrication problems gave this metal a bad reputation. For this reason, titanium hasn't yet seen its full potential in the bicycle industry. Titanium is still extremely popular in the aerospace industry. And contrary to popular belief, titanium is not too terribly expensive, not for highest quality bicycle frames and components. Look for titanium alloys to stage a comeback in the high-end market.

Molded and Other Advanced Composites: The principles of this process are described in the section on composites. This material has proven itself for use in high level competition. Don't be surprised if the price of molded composite frames drop into the range where they are competitive with traditional steel and aluminum frames. There is also much potential for other bicycle components to be mass produced from these strong and lightweight molded composites. Advanced Composite Technology, Inc., of Golden, Colorado, foresees the day when very little of a bicycle will necessarily be made with metal. This company expects to have composite frame lugs on their first production framesets. With fabrication economies of scale, these composites can be produced for mass produced bicycles.

Quantum Composites, Inc., of Midland, Michigan, is presently producing many structural parts for the aerospace and auto industries from Lytex. Lytex is Quantum Composite's proprietary glass fiber/epoxy resin composite that is compression molded into sheet, threaded connectors, automobile rims, and a number of other applications. This company has expressed a genuine interest in finding cycling applications for their material that would provide comparable strength to aluminum at two-thirds the weight and a lower cost.

Plastics and Other High Polymers: Plastics are already being used for applications where very high strength isn't needed. Brake and shift levers are often made of plastics. The big chemical companies like DuPont and Celanese are spending a great deal of money on research and development in this area. Several of the high strength nylons are already replacing metals for structural uses in many industries, especially the auto industry. Delrin ST, a product of DuPont, is claimed to be the world's toughest metal-like engineering plastic, and is expected to replace metals in many auto, consumer, and industrial applications. The potential for use in the bicycle industry is obvious.

GLOSSARY

TERMS AND DEFINITIONS

acid pickling: Immersion of metal into an acid bath to chemically remove the surface oxides and fluxes from brazing.

adhesive bonding: A materials joining process in which an adhesive (glue, epoxy, etc.) is placed between the two surfaces and solidifies to bond the materials.

alloy: A substance having metallic properties and being composed of two or more chemical elements of which at least one is a metal. Most metals are used as alloys.

Almag: A trade name for one of the 2XXX series aluminum alloys. Almag contains 4% Cu, 0.7% Mn, and 0.7% Mg.

anisotropy: Literally "not the same in all directions". The characteristic of exhibiting different values of a property in different directions or orientations. The mechanical properties of composites are highly anisotropic.

anodizing: Controlled oxidation of a metal surface by electrochemical action. A protective oxide layer is formed on the metal. The anodizing process is applied primarily to the aluminum alloys. (See "hard anodizing")

arc welding: A group of welding processes that fuse metals together by heating with an electric arc. (See "GTA welding")

Avional: A trade name for several similar aluminum alloys in the 2XXX series. Avional contains 2.5% to 5.0% copper and is heat treatable. Campagnolo uses Avional for many of their components.

brass: An alloy consisting mainly of copper (over 50%) and zinc. There are many different compositions of brass. Brass alloys are used for brazing of steel frame tubes, either with lugs or as fillet-brazed joints.

brazing: A process that joins metals by heating them to a suitable temperature, introducing a non-ferrous filler metal that melts and flows between the closely fitted joint, and then solidifies to form a strong bond. Unlike with welding, the base metals (tubing and lugs) do not melt in brazing. Soldering is very similar to brazing but is done at a lower temperature (below 450° C, or 840° F).

brinelling: Evenly spaced dents in a bearing raceway that occur when the bearing assembly is subjected to a force or impact load great enough to cause the ball bearings to indent the races.

brittle: An adjective describing a material's inability to deform plastically before fracturing. Brittle is the opposite of ductile, and brittle materials have low ductility.

bronze: A family of alloys consisting of mainly copper (over 50%) and tin. Bronzes aren't used for brazing, but brasses are.

butted tubing or butted spokes: Tubing or spokes that are made thinner in the center section than at the ends. (See "double butting")

carbon fiber: Thin, hair-like fibers of pure carbon that are used as the reinforcement material for carbon fiber composites. These fibers, by themselves, have extremely high tensile strengths, much greater than any metal.

Carpental: A trade name for a particular 5XXX series aluminum alloy. It is non-heat treatable.

case hardening: A generic term covering several processes that harden the surface of steel by absorption of carbon or nitrogen into the surface layer.

casting: Pouring molten metal into a mold to produce an object of desired shape. If a metal is not a cast product, then it is a wrought product. (Compare with "wrought product")

cast iron: A generic term for a large family of iron-based alloys that usually contain 2% to 4% carbon and 1% to 3% silicon. They are used in their cast form, i.e., not rolled, extruded, or similarly processed.

ceramics: One of the major groups of engineering materials. Glasses, cements, and bricks are all families of ceramics. Ceramics are not metals and visa-versa. There is very little use for ceramics in the bicycle industry.

cold forged: A forging process that is done at or near room temperature. This cold works the metal, thereby hardening and strengthening it as a result of forging. (See "forging" and "cold working")

cold setting: This term refers to bending or straightening of a metal, especially frame tubing, without heating the metal. (See "cold working")

cold working: Permanently deforming a metal at low temperatures so that the metal hardens in the region of cold working. When a metallic structure is cold worked, the metal strain hardens. Bicycle tubing and rims greatly rely on this phenomenon to achieve higher strengths.

compliance: A property of a material describing the amount of elastic strain that occurs per unit stress when loaded. Compliance is identical or nearly identical to resilience. (See "resilience", "elasticity", and "modulus of elasticity")

composites: Generally, a material that results when two or more materials, usually having different characteristics, are combined in order to provide the composite with useful properties for a specific application. In the world of bikes, this term usually refers to graphite fiber reinforced composites.

corrosion: The deterioration of a metal by chemical or electrochemical reaction with its environment. There are eight basic forms of corrosion. General corrosion of steel produces iron oxide, also known as "rust".

die forged: A forging whose shape is determined by impressions or patterns in specially prepared dies. (See "forging")

double-butting: A bicycle frame tube making process which produces tubing that is thicker at the ends than in the middle. Alfred M. Reynolds, of Reynolds tubing fame, invented this process in 1887. Most high-quality bike frames are made from butted tubing.

drop forged: A shallow forging made with impression dies, usually with a drop hammer. (See "forging")

ductility: The ability of a material to permanently deform without fracturing. The ductility of a metal or alloy is one of the mechanical properties important to know for structural design. Ductility is usually reported as percent elongation. A ductile material is the opposite of a brittle one.

Dural, duralumin, or duraluminum: This is a term that refers to the class of 2XXX series aluminum alloys that contain 4% to 6% copper. Occasionally, this term will refer to the specific alloy 2014. Alfred Wilm invented this alloy in 1906, in Berlin. Duralumin was the first heat treatable aluminum alloy.

Duralinox: This term may mean two different things: 1) A specific 5XXX series aluminum alloy containing 4.5% Mg. This alloy was formerly called "Alumag". 2) The combination of Dural (an aluminum alloy), and inox (French for stainless steel).

Durex: A trade name of the Italian rim manufacturer, Ambrosio. In Italian, durezza translates as "hardness".

elastic deformation: A change in shape that is proportional to the force applied to a material. Any and all elastic deformation is returned to the metal after the load is removed. All metals will deform elastically until they start to plastically (permanently) deform.

elasticity: The ability to deform elastically. A metal's modulus of elasticity characterizes how it will deform under load. (See "elastic deformation" and "modulus of elasticity")

electroplating: Depositing a metal or alloy upon the surface of another metal, using electric current to make this electrochemical reaction occur. Chrome plating is a form of electroplating.

endurance limit: When concerned with fatigue life, this is the maximum stress below which a material can presumable endure an infinite number of stress cycles. Steel alloys have endurance limits, but aluminum alloys do not. (See "fatigue strength")

epoxy or epoxy resin: Epoxies are a family of polymers that are used either as an adhesive for bonding frame tubing, or as the matrix that holds the fibers together in composites.

Ergal: A trade name for a high strength aluminum alloy in the 7XXX series. The common alloy 7075 is the equivalent of Ergal.

fatigue: The phenomenon in materials that leads to fracture under repeated or fluctuating stresses having a maximum value less than the tensile strength of the material. Fatigue is possibly the most common cause of premature failure of engineering structures.

fatigue strength: The maximum stress that can be sustained for a specific number of loading cycles without failure. Since aluminum alloys don't have an endurance limit, they have a fatigue strength reported, usually for 500 million cycles of loading. (See "endurance limit")

ferrous alloys: Alloys that are based on the metal iron. All steel alloys, from plain carbon steel to stainless steels, are ferrous alloys. (Compare with "nonferrous alloys")

filler metal: In the processes of brazing and welding, filler metal is the alloy that flows at high temperatures and forms a solid bond between the base metals. Brasses and silver alloys are common brazing filler metals for bike frame construction.

furnace brazing: A mass production brazing process in which the filler metal is preplaced on the joint, then the entire assembly is heated to the brazing temperature in a furnace. This is also known as "hearth brazing".

gas welding: A group of welding processes that fuse metals together with the heat of a gas flame. Oxy-acetylene welding is the most common of these processes.

grain size: This is a measure of the average size of grains in a metal. Generally, all metals consist of many microscopic crystals called grains. The grain size is important in determining mechanical properties of a metal and can be changed by thermomechanical processing.

graphite: The form of pure carbon that is used for carbon fiber. The words graphite and carbon are often used interchangeably when referring to carbon fiber composites.

GTA welding: Gas-Tungsten-Arc welding. This is the newer, more official term that replaces the term "TIG welding". A non-consumable electrode is used with an inert shielding gas (usually argon) for this type of arc welding.

hard anodizing: A type of anodizing process that produces a hard and thick oxide layer on the surface of aluminum. (See "anodizing")

hardness: Resistance of a metal to permanent (plastic) deformation, usually by indentation. The relative hardness of metals can be accurately measured with a standard hardness test, such as the Rockwell, Brinell, or Vickers tests. Hardness gives a rough estimate of the strength of a metal.

heat-affected zone (HAZ): The portion of the base metal that was not melted during brazing or welding, but whose microstructure and mechanical properties were altered by the heat.

heat treatable aluminum alloys: Those aluminum alloys that can be strengthened by specific heat treatments. The 2XXX, 6XXX, and 7XXX series aluminum alloys are all heat-treatable.

heat treated steel: Though, technically, all steel has been heat treated to a particular condition, this term describes steel that has been heat treated to obtain its highest strength level, usually by a quenching and tempering process. (See "Q & T Steel")

heat treatment: Heating and cooling a solid metal or alloy in such a way as to obtain desired conditions or properties. Not all processes that occur at elevated temperatures are classified as heat treatments.

heli-arc welding: Arc welding using a helium shielding torch gas. This produces a higher are temperature than with argon gas shielding. (See "TIG welding" or "arc welding")

high-tension steel: Also known as "high tensile steel", this is simply low carbon steel and is used for many low to medium priced bicycle framesets.

hydrogen embrittlement: A detrimental condition of low ductility in steels resulting from the absorption of hydrogen. Hydrogen can be introduced into the metal from one or more of the steps in the electroplating process. Hydrogen embrittlement becomes more of a concern in the very high strength steels. Titanium alloys may also be severely embrittled by hydrogen introduced during welding if the hot titanium is not adequately shielded.

Inox: This is a French term for stainless steel. It can also specifically refer to the 400 series stainless steels.

investment casting: Also called "lost-wax casting", this is a very precise and relatively expensive casting method usually used for high quality frame lugs and dropouts. A mold is produced by surrounding a wax or plastic pattern with molding compound. The pattern is melted or burned out of the mold before the metal is poured into this mold.

iron: The basic constituent in all steels. Chemical symbol Fe.

Kevlar: A DuPont trademark for their aramid polyester fiber with high strength and damage tolerance. Kevlar can be woven into a fabric and used for structural purposes. It is often mixed in with the carbon fibers in carbon fiber composites.

low alloy steel: Steels that contain up to 5% total alloy additions. Reynolds 753, 531, and Columbus SL, SP, SLX, are all low alloy steels.

Mangaloy: A trade name of the Japanese bicycle tube producer, Tange. This is a low carbon, high manganese steel.

matrix: The part of a composite that binds the fibers together. The matrix of carbon fiber composites is usually an epoxy.

mechanical properties: The properties of a material that reveal its elastic and inelastic behavior when force is applied, thereby indicating its suitability for mechanical applications. The mechanical properties of an alloy can be dramatically changed by various thermomechanical processes.

metal-matrix composites (MMC): A group of composites that use metal as the matrix instead of the familiar epoxy resin matrix. These composites are still very new and expensive. Consequently, they aren't yet used in the bicycle industry. Carbon fiber- reinforced aluminum is a common MMC used in the aerospace industry.

microstructure: The structure of metals on the microscopic level. Metal microstructures are revealed by examination of the etched surface of a polished specimen under a microscope. Metallurgists must be concerned with microstructures in order to understand and explain the mechanical behavior of metals.

mild steel: Plain carbon steel with a maximum of 0.25% carbon. Mild steel is also called low carbon steel. 1010 and 1020 are common mild steel alloys.

modulus of elasticity: This physical property measures the rigidity of metals. The higher the modulus, the more rigid the metal. For tensile loading, this property is also called Young's modulus and is given the symbol "E". The modulus of elasticity is constant for all alloys within an alloy system. All steels have a modulus of 30 million psi. All titanium alloys have a modulus of 17 million psi. And all aluminum alloys have a modulus of 11 million psi.

molded composites: This is a method of composite frameset construction that uses hand layups and two matched dies that are bonded together. This method, also called matched-die molding, is still quite new, very labor intensive, and expensive.

nonferrous metals: All of the metals and alloys that are not based on the metal iron. Aluminum, titanium, magnesium, gold, silver, etc., are all nonferrous metals.

plain carbon steel: Also known as carbon steel, this group of steels has carbon as the primary alloying element. Low carbon steel (0.01% to 0.25% C), medium carbon steel (0.25% to 0.60% C), and high carbon steel (greater than 0.60% C), are all plain carbon steels.

plain-gauge tubing: (See "straight-gauge tubing").

plastic deformation: Deformation that remains permanent after removal of the load that caused it. Plastic deformation will occur in a metal once the metal's yield strength is reached. (Compare with "elastic deformation")

polymer: A chemical substance, often organic, composed of multiple repetitive chains of atoms or groups of atoms, especially hydrogen, carbon, and oxygen. Polymers are used in many different types of composites.

quenched & tempered (Q & T) steel: Steel that has been heat treated to very high strength. Tange Prestige and Reynolds 753 are both Q & T steels.

Recidal: A trade name for the heat treatable aluminum-copper (2XXX series) alloy with the designation 2011.

resilience: The capacity of a metal, by virtue of high strength and low modulus of elasticity, to exhibit elastic deformation upon release of load. This means that for a steel alloy and an aluminum alloy with approximately the same yield strength, the aluminum will be more resilient because it has one-third the elastic modulus of steel. (See "compliance")

resin: A polymeric compound that is used as an adhesive. Epoxies are a family of resins. (See "polymer" and "epoxy resin")

rigidity: The rigidity of a bicycle frame or component describes its ability to resist bending or torsional loads. There are mathematical formulas to quantify rigidity; and they depend upon both the modulus of elasticity (stiffness) of the material and the geometry of the structure.

Rockwell hardness test: An indentation hardness test based on the depth of penetration of a specified penetrator into the specimen under a standard loading condition.

seamless tubing: Tubing that is fabricated without leaving a longitudinal seam. By contrast, seamed tubing is fabricated by rolling a strip of steel and welding it along its seam.

silver brazing: Brazing with a silver-base filler metal. There are several different types of silver braze alloys, each with a different chemical composition. Although this process is often called "silver soldering", silver brazing is the correct term.

soldering: Identical to brazing, except for the lower temperature of this process (lower than 450° C, or 840° F).

stainless steel: A family of steels that contain a high percentage of chromium (at least 10% Cr) and often nickel. Because of this large amount of chromium, stainless steels are highly corrosion resistant.

steel: A chemical combination of primarily iron with up to 2% carbon and varying amounts of other metal additions. There are a wide variety of steels that are further broken down into groups such as: carbon steels, low alloy steels, stainless steels, tool steels.

stiffness: A non-specific term that describes the resistance of a frame or component to elastic deformation. A measure of a particular metal's bending stiffness without concern for the geometry of the part is the modulus of elasticity. (Compare with "rigidity")

stress: The force (load, weight) per unit area. Stress is usually expressed in units of pounds-per-square-inch, psi. The term "strength" is often used interchangeably with stress.

stress raiser: Changes in the contour or dimension of a bicycle frame or component. When stress raisers are present, normal loads can create excessively high stresses in the region of a stress raiser. Fatigue failures most often occur at stress raisers. Notches, grooves, threads, and holes are common stress raisers in bicycles.

straight-gauge tubing: Also called "plain-gauge tubing", this bicycle tubing has a single constant wall thickness throughout the entire tube length. (Contrast with "butted tubing")

taper-gauge tubing: Bicycle frame tubing that has a gradually increasing wall thickness along its length.

temper: 1) In heat treatment, reheating hardened steel for the purpose of decreasing hardness (brittleness) and increasing toughness (See "toughness"); 2) For the aluminum alloys, this term refers to the heat-treated condition of an alloy. -O, -T4, and -T6 are common aluminum temper designations.

tensile strength: In tensile testing, the maximum stress that a material can withstand before breaking. This mechanical property is also known as the ultimate tensile strength, UTS, or TUS. (Compare with "yield strength")

tensile testing: One of the most widely used means of evaluating the engineering properties of metals. A specimen of standard dimensions is slowly pulled apart in tension until it fractures. Results of this mechanical test are yield strength, ultimate tensile strength, and percent elongation.

thermomechanical processing: A general term covering a variety of processes combining controlled thermal (heating and cooling) and deformation treatments to produce desired mechanical properties in a metal. Same as thermal-mechanical working.

TIG welding: Tungsten-Inert-Gas welding. (See "GTA welding")

toughness: The ability of a metal to absorb energy and deform plastically before fracturing. Toughness is a necessary property for metals that sustain high impact loads. A material that has very low toughness is "brittle".

ultimate tensile strength, UTS: (See "tensile strength").

welded tubing: Bicycle frame tubing that is rolled from sheet into a tubular shape and welded along the seam. (Compare with "seamless tubing")

welding: Joining two or more pieces of metal by applying heat so that the base metals are melted and fused together. Filler metal may or may not be used. The two most common welding techniques are arc welding and gas welding. Weldability is a measure of a material's ability to be welded. Some metals are easily welded while some have poor weldability and aren't usually welded.

work hardening: An increase in strength and hardness caused by plastic deformation at relatively low temperatures (less than one-half of the melting temperature). Extruding, cold rolling, cold forging, and stamping are just some examples of metal fabrication processes that cause work hardening. Also called strain hardening. (See "cold working")

wrought products: Parts that are produced by working a solid metal either hot or cold; for example, by forging, rolling, stamping, drawing, extruding, etc. (Compare with "casting")

yield strength, YS: The stress at which a material starts to plastically deform. The yield point marks where elastic deformation turns to plastic deformation (the elastic limit of the material has been exceeded). Also known as tensile yield strength, TYS. (See "tensile testing" and "elasticity")

Zicral: A trade name of Pechiney Metal Works (France) that refers to the equivalent of the aluminum alloy 7075.

References and Additional Reading

American Bicyclist And Motorcyclist, Cycling Press, Inc., N.Y., N.Y.

Bicycle Dealer Showcase Magazine, Magacycle, Inc., Cleveland, Ohio

Bicycle Guide Magazine, Raben/Bicycle Guide Partners, Boston, MA

Bicycling Magazine, Rodale Press, Inc., Emmaus, PA

Bicycling Science, F. R. Whitt and D. G. Wilson, MIT Press, 1985

Bike Tech, Rodale Press, Inc., Emmaus, PA

The Custom Bicycle, Michael J. Kolin, Denise M. de la Rosa, Rodale Press, Inc., 1979

Materials Engineering Magazine

Metals Handbook, American Society for Metals

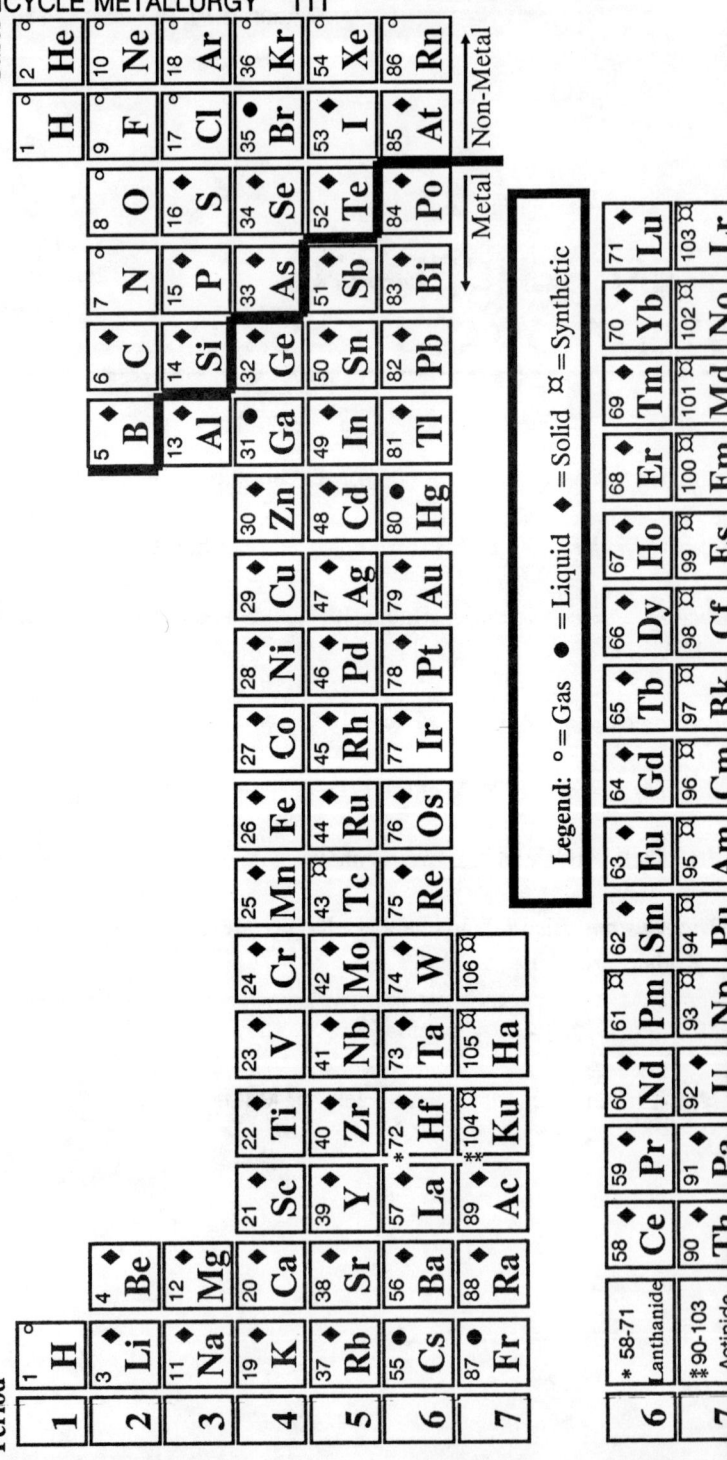